A Treatise on the Affections

William Fenner

CONTENTS

To the Reader:

God made man (as all things else) for himself; God's glory is the end for which man was made; the fruition of God is the happiness to which he was appointed; that he might be subservient to this end, and obtain this happiness, he bestowed on him a reasonable soul, consisting of an understanding and a will, that by the one he might contemplate and behold the beauty of the Lord by the other he might embrace him. The understanding as the eye of the soul to discern truth, the will as the feet of the soul to carry it to good. The understanding (though furnished with excellent knowledge in things natural) was chiefly enriched with the knowledge of God the first Truth; the will (though let out to the desire of good natural) was especially enamoured with God the chiefest good; and whilst these faculties continued in those postures, man continued in the happy and holy condition of his primaeval creation; the corruption and misery of the soul is the aversion of these faculties from this object, the corruption of the understanding, the ignorance of God; the corruption of the will, the abhorring of God; man lost not his faculties by his fall, but their integrity; he hath an understanding still, but in regard of heavenly things blind and vain, quick-sighted in other things, he hath a will still, but averse from God, and pursuing with eagerness things terrene; the reparation of the soul is the resetting of these faculties on their proper objects, and this is that which is required, "My son, give me thy heart, give me thy understanding to know me, give me thy will to cleave to me, by loving and fearing me, by delighting and hoping in me." These acts of loving, fearing, &c. commonly called by the name of Affections (I speak with submission to better judgments) are only the motions of the will, by which it goes forth to the embracing of its object which is Good; which considered in the general nature is loved, considered as in the fruition is delighted in; considered in the future as attainable, if with ease, is desired; if with difficulty, is hoped for. If the will or these Affections be fixed on their proper object, there is no danger in the excess; God cannot be loved, or feared, &c. overmuch; the only danger in them is either in misplacing upon a wrong object, or their loose adhering to the right; both these the Apostle rectifies, "Be not drunk with Wine, in which is excess, but be filled with the Spirit, Covet the best gifts." Thus Christ invites his Church, "Drink ye, be drunk, O my beloved." This drunkenness, saith Ambrose, makes men sober: And this is the subject of this ensuing Discourse published for thy benefit. Read, consider, pray, and the Lord give thee understanding to conceive of it, and a will to conform unto it.

The First Sermon.

"Set your affections on things that are above, and not on things which are on the earth." – Colossians 3:2

The subject of the Text and this Treatise is the affections, showing the right use and ordering of them, which is a thing of continual and great concernment: for they will never be idle, but still running out and bringing into the soul, either healing or hurtful objects, and so authors either of our woe or welfare: and certain signs either of our happiness, that we are risen with Christ: or misery, that we are still dead. —And concerning these the Apostle

First, Implies a disease and distemper: that they are disjoined from God, and that desperately.

Secondly, Applies a medicine, a way to cure them, to bring them back, and place them upon their first and right object, God, and things above.

The first he intimates to us in three things.

First, By calling them inordinate affections, and such as can never be set right without they be mortified. "Mortify your earthly members, Fornication, Uncleanness, Inordinate affection," &c. ver. 5. He terms them inordinate and masterless affections, and he commands us to mortify them.

Secondly, By showing they are buried in the things of the world, and never can be raised up again, but only by the power of the resurrection of Christ, "If ye be risen with Christ, seek those things that are above," ver. 1. Ye can never be able to make your affections seek upwards, unless ye be risen with Christ.

Thirdly, By supposing they are naturally (as Solomon says of a fool's wrath) as heavy as a stone; the affections are so naturally, as heavy as a stone, which falls down to the earth, and cannot ascend, except it be heaved up: "Set your affections on things above, and not on things on the earth." They naturally sag downwards on things that are earthly, but let them not do so: no, heave them up, and set them upon things that are heavenly, "If you be risen with Christ."

These words are to be construed with all the exhortations Saint Paul doth here give, "If ye be risen with Christ, seek those things that are above, If ye be risen with Christ, set your affections on things that are above, If ye be risen with Christ, mortify your earthly members, and your inordinate affections," &c. If ye be not risen with Christ, it is but folly for me to bid you do this; ye cannot mortify your affections, nor raise up your affections to God, ye cannot possibly do this, except ye be risen with Christ. The point then is this, which I will handle by way of coherence,

A natural man cannot set his affections upon God, or upon things above: For our more intelligible proceeding in this Doctrine, as likewise in the whole treatise of the affections, which I desire to go through: let me tell you,

First, What the affections be. The affections are the forcible and sensible motions of the heart or the will, to a thing or from a thing, according as it is apprehended to be good or to be evil. There be four things to be considered herein.

First, The affections are motions. They are the motions of the heart. The motions of sin, says Saint Paul, Rom. 7:5. that is, the affections of sin, for so it is in the original: so that then are a man's affections set upon God, when the heart hath its out-goings to God, and therefore the Scriptures call the affections the feet of the soul: for as the body goes with its feet to that which it loves, so the soul goes out with its affections to that which it loves. "I thought upon my ways, and turned my feet unto thy testimonies," Psal. 119:59. that is, I turned mine affections to thy Testimonies: "Look to thy feet when thou comest into the house of the Lord." "I have refrained my foot from every evil way," Psal. 119:101. "Their feet are swift to shed blood," Rom. 3:15. The Soul hath no other way to come at that which it loves, but only by its affections: can the muck-worm bring his bags and his coffers to his Soul? Can the voluptuous man bring his dogs, and his hounds, and his bowls to his Soul? No, though his Soul loves such vanities as these, it cannot move to them but only by its affections, "Currui similes sunt & equis pernicibus affectus," says Lactantius. The affections are the Souls horses, that draw her as it were in a Coach to the thing that she affects: a man is moved by his affections. By Anger he moves out to revenge: by Desire he moves out to obtain: by Love he moves out to enjoy: by Pity he moves out to relieve: the affections are the motions of the Soul. When the unbelieving Jews had an affection of envy at Saint Paul, the Text says, "They were moved with Envy," Act. 17:5. so the Soul of the godly is moved with affection to God. This is the first thing, the affections are motions.

Secondly, As the affections are motions, so they are the motions of the will. I know Aristotle and most of our Divines too, do place the affections in the sensitive part of the Soul, and not in the will, because they are to be seen in the beasts. But this cannot be so, for a man's affections do most stir at a shame or disgrace; which could not be, if the affections were in the unreasonable sensitive part: the unreasonable sensitive part of a man is not sensible of credit or esteem: call the desires of the appetite greedy and gluttonish; the appetite is senseless of any disgrace, and therefore the affections must needs be in the heart: the Scripture places the affections in the heart or the will. "Being affectionately desirous of you, we were willing," 1 Thes. 2:8. Saint Paul couples his affections and his will together in one, and his affection that he had to the Thessalonians, he seats in his will. How could the Apostle command us to set our affections on God, and the things that are above, if the affections were in the sensitive and unreasonable part? Can a man make his material stomach to hunger after God? Or the thirst of his sensitive appetite to thirst after Christ? Alas the sensitive part is not capable of a command or precept. No, if the affections were only in the sensitive and material part of the soul, then how could they be in the Angels? The good Angels have affections, all the essential parts of the affections, and so have the bad. The good Angels, "Which things the Angels desire to look into," 1 Pe. 1:12. The evil Angels or Devils, "The Devils believe and tremble," Jam. 2:19. I confess there be certain animal and analogical affections that are in the sense: there's grief for torment, and fear to touch a serpent or a toad; delight in meats that are pleasant, and hatred of them that are noisome. But the Lord doth not call for these sensitive passions to be seated upon him and on heaven, they are seated aright as they stand, so a moderation be kept they have no need to change objects: The affections of the heart, these are the affections the Lord doth call for; the out-goings of the heart: as the sense is afraid of a Lion, so is a godly heart afraid to sin against God; as the sense is joyful to have ease after trouble, so a godly heart is joyful with a good conscience in Christ; as the sense loves that which doth feed it, so a godly heart loves

God that doth nourish it: and therefore Austin, and Galen, and Scotus, and why say I them? The Scriptures say, the affections are motions in the heart, "Mine Eye affecteth my heart," saith the poor Church, Lam. 3:51. that is, when she beheld the lamentable distresses of the daughters of Zion, this stirred up the affection of pity in her heart.

Thirdly, As the affections are the motions of the heart, so they are the forcible motions of the heart; every little motion in the heart is not an affection, but only the forcible motions of the heart; a man is then said to set his affections upon God when his heart goes with force unto God; for as God appoints every creature his task, and to seek out its own good, so he gives it a force to do it; the stone, its nature is to fall downwards, and God gives it a weightiness that it may fall downwards with force: the stomach, its nature is to take food when it is empty, and God gives it a hunger that it may take it with force: every creature hath not only its motion to move it to its own good, but it goes to it with force; so God hath given affections to the heart, as weight to the stone, and hunger to the stomach; so God I say hath given affections to the heart, that it may seek out its good with a force, so that then does a man set his affections upon God when he sets all his forces to Godward. When David had given £847,382,500 in silver and gold of his own charges to the building of God's house, for so the learned may gather out of two Chapters in the Chronicles, you may well think he employed all his forces thereto; but what says the Text, "I have set mine affection to the house of God." 1 Chron. 29:3. Thus ye see when the heart sets his affections to God's house, he put to his forces: the affections are the forcible motions of the heart; when a child of God prays with affection he prayeth with force; when he stands for God with affection, he stands for him with force.

Fourthly, As the affections are the motions, and the forcible motions of the will, so they are the sensible motions too. For the will stirs up the inferior faculties of the Soul, and they stir up the humours and parts of the body, to make the greater resistance to that which it disaffects, or the greater embracement of that which it affects.

This is one reason why the affections are called passions, for they make the soul to suffer, and the body to suffer. The affection of Joy makes the spleen to suffer, and anger makes the gall to suffer, and fear makes the heart to suffer; yea, the affections make humours, blood, spirits, members, even bones and all the body to suffer. Hence it is, when a man sets his affections upon God, his fear of God makes him tremble; his Love, the love of God makes him to weep for his sins; the shame of it that he should dishonour his God, makes him to blush before Christ; Grief for his sins many times dries up his moisture; and Zeal for his glory consumeth his flesh: so was it with the Psalmist, when he was full of affections towards God, and saw how men did disobey his Commandments, see what sensible motions were in him, "Mine eyes gush out with rivers of waters, because men keep not thy Law," Psalm. 119:139. Ezra was so affectionate for God, that knowing how the people transgressed, it made the colour to come in his face, and to blush before heaven, Ezr. 9:6. as Demetrius blushed for his father Philip's offences; the Orator that pleaded King Philip's defence, did not do him so much service, as the blushing of Demetrius his son. This was the effect of his affection to his Father, it showed itself in his blushing for the offences of his Father: Thus the affections are the sensible motions of the Will.

Fifthly and lastly, They are such sensible motions as are according to the apprehension of good or evil. For when there is but small apprehension of good or evil, the affections are weak, and may hardly work on the body at all; but when there is a great apprehension of either, not only the soul is deeply affected, but also the body is mightily compatible. Nay, if the apprehension be deep indeed, the affections break out into raptures, as dancings and leapings of the heart, which are the raptures of joy: ravishments and enamourings, which are the raptures of love; meltings and bleedings, and breakings of spirit, which are the raptures of grief; astonishments, amazements, which are the raptures of fear; confusion and the like, which are the raptures of shame; the affections burst forth into such raptures as these, when the apprehension is deep. Olofernes his eyes were ravished with the slippers of Judith, because he was deeply in love with her: Jacob shaken almost dead at the sight of his son's bloody coat, because he was deeply affected thereat. The Roman Senate were affrighted at the sight of the Carthaginian green figs, that Cato did show them: such raptures have the Saints very often in their prayers to God, being helped with sighs and groans that cannot be uttered, Rom. 8:26. because they have a deep apprehension of the corruption that is in them. Thus ye see what the affections be, they are forcible and sensible motions of the will, to a thing or from a thing, according as it is apprehended to be evil or to be good.

In the next place, let me show that a carnal man cannot set his affections upon God or upon Grace, which may appear by Reasons.

First, Affectus sunt alae animae, as the Proverb goes, "The Affections are the wings of the soul." If the bird's wings be lime-twigged and glued to the ground, she cannot fly up; now a carnal man, his affections are glued and lime-twigged to the things of the world, or the things of this life; and therefore it is impossible he should fly up unto God. I read in the life of good Anselm, walking in the fields he saw a shepherd's boy that had taken a bird, and tied a stone to her leg, and as the bird would be offering to mount, the stone pulled her down; she had such a weight on her leg, she could not fly up: this good father fell a weeping, to consider, that so it was with men, carnal men; though perhaps they think to fly up to God by many good purposes, they are still borne down with their sins, their affections are clogged, security, deadness of heart, self-love, and love of the things here below, like millstones made fast to their heels, their affections cannot mount up to God. Hast thou more affection to a game than a Sermon? More affection to sit drinking in Ale-houses, than to be reproved for thy sins? More affection to a good booty, than a good duty? Alas! How canst thou set thine affections upon God? Thine affections are earthly affections, and therefore they cannot be placed upon God. In Romans 1:26, we read of vile affections. God gave up the Heathen to base and vile affections: so these are base and vile, and carnal affections, that thou art given unto: thine affections are malice, and envy, and revenge, which cannot be set upon God: they are worldly fears, and worldly sorrows, and worldly joys, and worldly pleasures, and worldly delights, these are thine affections, these can never be placed upon God. They are vile affections, too base and dishonourable to God. Thine affections are lime-twigged by Satan, they cannot soar up unto God. This is the first reason why a carnal man cannot set his affections upon God, because his affections, which are the wings of his soul, are glued to the earth.

Secondly, Affectus sunt inclinationes animae, "The affections are the inclinations of the Soul": as a man is affected so he is inclined; and therefore the affections in Scripture are called the bent of the soul, "My people are bent to backsliding from me," Hosea 11:7. that is, their affections to me are unstable, inconstant and fickle. How stands such a one bent? As we say; that is, how stands he affected? A man is bent to that which his affections are on; now then is it possible that a carnal man should set his affections on God, when his heart does not stand bent unto God? The muck-worm, his heart stands bent to the world, the voluptuous his heart stands bent to his pleasures; the proud man, his heart stands bent to get credit and be well thought on; the natural man stands bent to be carnal and earthy, and how can such men set their affections on God, when their hearts stand that way bent? Are thy affections bent? That way that thy bent goes, that way do thine affections go: Thou art merry and jocond, and joyful today, tell me what is it for? Is it because God is glorified by thee? No, No, thy mirth and thy joy stand otherwise bent. Thou hast been angry and revengeful, what was it for? Was it because God is dishonoured, and thy lusts have been violent? Alas no, thy anger and thy wrath stand otherwise bent: thine affections are the bent and inclinations of thy heart, and therefore if thou be inclined to things that are earthy, thou canst not place thine affections upon God; nothing can go against its own bent and inclination, unless by the omnipotent power of the Spirit of Christ. David knew this well enough, that his affections could never be to God and his righteousness, if his heart did not that way stand bent; and therefore he prays God, "Incline not my heart to any evil thing," Psalm 141:4. Let not mine affections be on any evil thing, for then I should be that way inclined. This is the second reason why a carnal man cannot set his affections upon God, because the affections of the heart are the bent of the heart.

Thirdly, Affectus sunt passiones animae, says Damascene, "The affections are the passions of the Soul." When the heart is affected with a thing, it lets in that thing, and it suffers a change by that thing; when a man is affected with anger at a wrong or an injury, we say he is in a passion; that is, he lets in the wrong, and there does his heart bite upon the wrong, and chafe at it; thus he is passionate: When a man is affected with love to a pleasure, he lets in the pleasure, and suffers it to prevail on the heart: now then a carnal man cannot set his affections upon God nor his Grace, because he cannot let it in to prevail over his Soul, he will not suffer it to enter; can he be in a good passion for God? Can he be angry and choleric to see how God's Spirit is grieved? Can he be grieved at the lusts of his heart, which he joys in? Can he be zealous for God's truth, and for the beauty of holiness? Alas, alas! No, He cannot let in these things into his heart, nor Christ, nor grace, nor holiness, nor humility, nor self-denial, nor any saving grace that is Christ's, can get entrance into his heart; and therefore he cannot set his affections upon God. When the Apostle had exhorted the Hebrews, and now was concluding, that he could exhort them no further, he concludes on this manner: "And I beseech you brethren, suffer the word of exhortation," Hebrews 13:22. He labours to work on their affections, that they would let in his exhortations into their hearts, he does not say, Suffer me to exhort you, for he had exhorted them already, and had taken their leave, but suffer it to enter into your hearts; now if you be carnal, thou wilt never suffer God's counsels to enter; you will never suffer the word of reproof, neither will ye suffer a resignation: Suppose we should pull down all the unnecessary Ale-houses in the Parish, would ye suffer it? Suppose we should root out all your game-houses and the like, would ye suffer it? Suppose we should make every man pay his 12. pence a day for every time he is absent from Church, and have all disorders punished in the Town, would ye suffer it? Suppose we should come to your houses and exhort you, and reprove you, and tell you of your sins, and labour to reform you and your families, alas! Would ye suffer it? No, your passions will rise, ye would be so far from affecting these things, as that your affections would be against them, nay, ye would be in passion against me; carnal hearts cannot set their affections upon God, why? Because the affections are passions, as I have proved already, and the soul doth suffer its affections. The affections do alter the heart, but a carnal heart will not be altered by the word, nor by Christ; nor suffer his graces to enter.

Fourthly, Put the case a man set himself wrong, Affectus sunt perturbationes animae, "The affections are the perturbations of the Soul";

if once they go wrong, and the reins be laid on their necks, they are like wild horses to the soul, to carry her wherever she would not; they are the disturbers of judgment, and violent tyrants over the soul, they make a man walk as they list; and therefore the Apostle calls them, the lusts of concupiscence, wherein a man walks, 1 Thessalonians 4:5. In the original it is the affections of concupiscence, they are cruel and masterless misleaders of a man; now a carnal man, his affections are such, they are disturbances and perturbations unto him, they will so trouble him, and toss him up and down, from lust unto lust, from sin unto sin, that he shall never be able, that is carnal, to set them upon God. Iamblichus calls them the nails of the soul, whereby it's nailed to the things of the body; would a carnal man repent? Alas! His affections disturb him; would he pray and hold out in that duty? His affections are importunate to be otherwise occupied; would he exhort and reprove, and be rebuking his neighbour for sinning against God? His affections they are against it, he is ashamed for to do it, he is afraid he shall have a flout for his labour; would he forsake his covetousness and drunkenness and company? Oh, his affections are so strong to them, that he is not able to draw his heart from them. The very Heathen bring in all the world thus speaking of themselves, nitimur in vetitum semper cupimusque negata, so headstrong are the affections when they are wrong: as Medea in the Poet, "video meliora proboque," she saw the good and she liked the good, but her affections transported her quite to the contrary; thus it was with Herod the king: when he heard there was another king of the Jews born in the world, and that Wise men from the East were come for to do homage to that new King; the Text says, he was troubled, Matthew 2:3. fear and shame, and grief, and vexation, and all his affections, they were all up in arms, and would not let him be quiet: they troubled him, says Saint Matthew. Yea, they made such a disturbance in Herod, they did so baffle his judgment, and busy his thoughts, and torture his mind, that they drove him to murder God knows how many scores of poor Infants: before they would be quiet, they made him a mad man. Thus the affections are grievous perturbations, when they are once misplaced; and if they be such perturbations as they are, alas! How can a carnal man set his affections upon God? They are masterless wild horses, and he cannot subdue them: they are bedlams and frantic misleaders, and he cannot overcome them: they are desperate things, his affections are so giddy and unruly, that he can never be Christ's, as long as his affections are alive; unless they be set upon the tenters, and put upon the wreck, and tamed perforce, they will never be right: and therefore says the Apostle, "Those that are Christ's have crucified the flesh, with the affections and lusts," Galatians 5:24. Those that are Christ's have done so, or else they could never be Christ's, because the affections are perturbations and disturbances, most woeful perturbations they are. And this is a fourth reason why a carnal man cannot set his affections upon God, because his affections are perturbations, and like a company of wild horses, that will not be ruled.

The Second Sermon.

"Set your affections on things that are above, and not on things which are on the earth." – Colossians 3:2

Thus I have shown you First, what the affections are: Secondly, how a carnal man cannot set his affections upon God. But here it may be objected: Cannot a carnal man have good affections to God and to grace? The people were so affected with John's preaching, and with his baptism, that they would have been angry and zealously affected against that man, whoever he was that should have said it was not of God; they would have stoned such an one to death, Luke 20:6. Most of the people were carnal, yet they were thus affected with his preaching. Certainly, a carnal man's affections may be marvelously wrought on. For the clearing of this doubt: Let me show you nine degrees, wherein the affections may be wrought on: in five of them, a carnal man may have his affections to be wrought on, and in the last four of them he cannot. First, I will name you these nine degrees of the affections of the heart.

The first is when they are so far wrought on, that the heart is enticed and allured much by them. Thus the eloquent Ministers in Corinth, it seems they wrought upon the people's affections exceedingly, their words were so drawing, and their speech was so enticing, that they came flocking to them. Saint Paul confesses he would not preach so, with the enticing words of men's wisdom, 1 Corinthians 2:4. What good should I do if my preaching were such? It's true I might allure you and move you, and entice you, and stir your affections; but alas! This would never bring you to faith and repentance with power: this might tickle your hearts perhaps a little, but not soundly comfort you.

The second is when the affections are wrought on so far, that the heart is somewhat touched therewith. As a man when his affections are moved with any, at a disgraceful word, he says, "this toucheth me indeed." When God turned the affections of Israel unto Saul, indeed some of them had no affection to Saul, "How shall this man save us?" say they, they despised him in their hearts, but God turned the affections of the rest upon Saul, for to follow him: The Text says of them, "The Lord hath touched their hearts," 1 Samuel 10:26. That is, he set their affections upon Saul, that they might follow Saul up and down. As when the Needle is touched with the Loadstone, then it will turn itself presently to the North; their affections were touched, and therefore they followed after Saul. So many men, their affections are touched at a Sermon; their affections are not only allured, but receive a touch from the Word: there is some virtue goes out of the Word, as some went from Christ to the Woman that had but a touch of his garment; so their affections have but a touch from the Word, and some virtue goes to them, for the affections are termed the touch of the heart. It's good for a man not to touch a woman, 1 Corinthians 7:1. That is, not to set an amorous affection of the heart upon a woman Thus far a wicked man's affections may be to the Word, they may be touched by the Word.

The third is when the affections are wrought on so far, That the heart is somewhat bowed thereby; this is another degree of working on the affections, to bow the affections, as ye may read; David bowed the heart of all the men of Judah, even as the heart of one man, 2 Samuel 19:14. That is, by his kind speeches, and friendly message he sent, he inclined and bowed their affections unto him. So a wicked man may have his affections bowed unto good, whereas his affections stood sturdy before, or maybe they were bowed another way before, now they be bowed the contrary; as wicked Joab's affections were so bowed to Godwards, and for the good of his Church, that he was willing to die in his defense. "Be of good courage" (says he) "let us play the men, for our people and the cities of our God; and the Lord do what seemeth him good," 2 Samuel 10:12. See how he rouses up his valour, and his generous affections to fight for his God, his affections were somewhat bowed unto God, and yet he was a wicked man.

The fourth is, The affections may be wrought on so far, that the heart may be stolen away with them: this you may find in the story of Absalom, who with his beauty and the propriety of his person, and the flattery of his lips, and his courteous compliment with the people of the land, he did so win their affections, that the Text says, He stole the hearts of the men of Israel, 2 Samuel 15:6. So grace is so beautiful, and the Word of God has such kind promises and kind speeches with it, not complementary, as Absalom's, but real and truly amiable, that it may steal the affections of a carnal man, as the Israelites stole from the Egyptians and they knew not how, so grace may steal thine affections and take them with its beauty, and yet thou be a wicked man for all that. As Paul with his preaching did so steal away the affections and the hearts of the Galatians, that for a need they would have plucked out their eyes and given them to Paul, they were so strongly affected with him, and the Gospel he taught them, Galatians 4:15. Nevertheless Saint Paul says they were foolish and carnal.

The fifth is, The affections may be wrought on so far, that the heart may be hot and inflamed by them. That this is another degree of the affections, you may gather from the avenger of blood; when any had unwittingly and unwillingly killed his brother, the Lord commands him to fly quickly to a City of refuge, lest the avenger of blood should kill him in fury and anger. The words go thus, lest the avenger of blood pursue the slayer, while his heart is hot, Deuteronomy 16:6. While his heart is hot, that is while he is in the heat of his passion, while his anger and the affections of revenge are hot: the affections may be raised so high, that they may set the heart in a heat upon a thing which it affects. So a carnal man may have his affections heated and inflamed towards God and towards grace. Saul had a great zeal for God's Church, 2 Samuel 21:2. Jehu was zealous for God, "Come with me" (says he) "and see my zeal for the Lord," 2 Kings 10:16. Zeal is the heat of all the affections, and therefore Jehu was heated in all his affections for God; his affections were hot to root out Idolaters, his affections were hot to cut off God's enemies, and to reform abundance of sinful abuses in the Kingdom: he was zealous, his affections were heated towards God, and yet Jehu was no better than a carnal man for all that. Thus far may a carnal man's affections be wrought on for grace; and this is no argument that he hath set his affections upon God as shall afterwards appear. Therefore there are four further degrees which are only to be found in the godly.

The sixth then is, The affections may be wrought on so far, that the heart is quite overturned from that it was before; I say the affections may be wrought on so far, that the heart may be turned upside down by them. So it was with the godly; they were even overwhelmed in affections for God with the fear of the Lord, and their hearts turned upside down with grief for their sins, "Behold O Lord, for I am in distress, my bowels are troubled, my heart is turned within me, for I have grievously rebelled," Lamentations 1:20. Her soul was even battered with affections of repentance and humiliation; her soul was distressed with terrors; her bowels were troubled and contracted with fears, and her heart was turned upside down with sorrows, and all for her sins, for I have grievously rebelled, says she. No wicked man under Heaven had his affections ever so wrought on, that was not converted upon it. As Job says of his birth, He was curdled like Cheese: so here in the second birth, her heart was curdled like Cheese, etc. "My heart is turned in me," says she. This is a higher working on the affections, then any carnal man hath.

The seventh is, The affections may be wrought on so far, that the heart be engaged for God. As a woman's affections towards a man may be so deep, as that she engageth her heart unto that man, and resolves to have none other husband but him. So when the affections are so deep in love with grace and with Christ, that the heart is once engaged for Christ, to be a widow forever, unless he will be pleased to count her his Spouse: the world shall never have her heart more, the flesh shall never have her heart more, nor devil, nor lust, nor any other sin shall ever have her heart more, she is so far in love and affection with Christ, as her heart is engaged for Christ, this is a godly soul. "Who is this that engageth his heart to approach unto me?" saith the Lord, Jeremiah 30:21. If pleasure come, saying, set thine affections on me; no, says the heart, mine affections are engaged already; if her old lusts, and her old lovers, and her old acquaintance come, saying, set your affections on us; no, says the heart, I am engaged for another, even for Christ and his graces: this is a deep working on the affections indeed, when they are engaged for Christ.

The eighth is, The affections may be wrought on so far, that the heart may be glued to a thing by them. Iamblichus the heathen hath a pretty phrase to this purpose: a wicked man he calls him ἐνεδραμών, bound in and nailed in his affections, he is even nailed and glued to the things of the world, his heart does even stick to them like pitch and Tar to the Ship. So it is with a godly soul, his heart sticks fast unto Christ, and the commandments of Christ. "I have stuck unto thy Testimonies," says David to Christ, Psalm 119:31. How came his heart to stick to Christ's testimonies? His holy affections were the glue, his affections clave to God's Law.

The ninth is, The affections may be wrought on so far, that the heart may be quite given up to the thing which it affects. Solomon had such affections to wisdom that he gave his heart to seek it, Ecclesiastes 1:13. As we use to say, he hath my heart, what can he have more? All mine affections are set on him, if he have my heart and all. So a godly heart is so deeply affected with Christ and his righteousness, as that Christ hath his very heart and all. He gives up all that he hath unto Christ. It's true, no wicked man in the earth hath his affections thus far wrought on: but it is marvelous to think how far a man's affections may be wrought on for Christ, and yet be a carnal man. It's proved already, he cannot set his affections on Christ, but he may raise up his affections a good way towards Christ, and now I will prove it.

First, the inclinations and embers of right reason, that God hath made natural to his heart, may regulate his affections to be chaste, and sober, and kind, and liberal, and just, and morally humble, and patient, and merciful, etc. and to observe the things contained in the Law. Natural reason directs men to love their parents and their children, and one another: thus the very Heathen themselves guided their affections with Religion as it were, the virtues of morality says Aristotle, they do μετριοπαθεῖν, They find out a Medium or a golden mean in the affections, and hold them unto it. And therefore Saint Paul knows thus much, and how that some of the Heathen were so wicked, that they would put out the light of their own reason, and be drunk and lustful, and proud, and merciless, and disobedient to parents, he condemns them especially for this, that they were without understanding, and without natural affection, Romans 1:31. that is, because they put out that natural reason, and that natural affection that were in them. Because their affections might have been naturally set upon those things. Their very natural reason might have ruled their affections, and set them upon virtues of morality. So that thus far thou mayest go, and yet be a carnalist, thine affections may run to be civil, and morally honest, and the like natural reason may raise up thine affections from drunkenness and lust, and from natural injustice, and from swearing and lying, and filthiness of speaking, and the like. I say, natural reason may raise up thine affections from these. Indeed it may be thine affections are violent and greedy, and sensual to tempt thee to some of these sins, but natural reason may take them off from such sins as these. Are thine affections so vile as to follow thy carousing and thy company-keeping? We need not quote Scripture to convince thee: thy material stomach cries out it is a sin, for it grumbles at it. Thine eyes and thy legs, and thy heels cry out, it's a sin; for they do betray it. Look upon thy purse, it cries against thee, for thou hast emptied it. Look upon thy Children, and thy Wife, they cry against it, for them thou hast beggared. Look upon thy fields and thy land, and thy inheritance, they cry against it, for them thou hast mortgaged and impaired. Look upon the stinking dunghill, it bids thee hold thy nostrils at the stinkiness of this sin, for there is thy spewing and thy vomiting, and so of the rest of these sins: natural reason may easily raise up thine affections from these. Which if thou hast done already, and art civil and moral, thou art yet gone no further than a Naturian may go. Thou mayest do that, and yet be a Carnalist.

Secondly, Because thou hast more means than the means of bare nature, thy knowledge out of the Word may raise up thy affections exceedingly: knowledge may awe the heart, and move it with the affection of fears, that it go not against its own knowledge. Herod feared John, knowing that he was a just man. Mark 6:20. Herod's affection was stirred with fear at the hearing of John; why? He knew he was a good man, and he knew it was just as he preached; he knew it was God's Word. And therefore he feared not to obey him, he was afraid to go against him. Nay, his affections were more raised than so; he heard John gladly and did many things. He was affected with joy at his Sermons, and his affections were wrought on to break out into act, and to do many things. I do not read he struck at anything but only his darling corruption. His affections were so wrought on, that it should seem he reformed many sins in his Court and many of his Courtiers; he began to set up some worship of God in his Palace. All this was by reason of knowledge; he knew John was a good Preacher, he knew he preached the truth, and the truth overpowered his affections. Now he had no such elbow-room for to sin, as he had in his ignorance. Now he fears to do many sins that before he feared not, why? Because his knowledge was enlightened. This is no argument that thou art a child of God, because thou reformest many things: Alas, thy knowledge is convinced thou must so: the very devil himself was overpowered by his knowledge; when the devil knew Christ was Christ, he could not but confess, "We know thee who thou art, the holy one of God." Mark 1:24. Happily thou fearest to go flatly against the Sermons thou hearest, thou fearest to live so bad as thou didst; happily thou rejoicest to hear the Bell ring to a Sermon, and art glad to hear the preaching of a Minister; happily thine affections are so wrought on, that thou art moved to do many things, not to suffer such potting and cupping in thy house as thou usedst, not to endure such disorders in thy family as thou wert wont; alas, alas, this is good yet; and O that others were proficiency thus far, this is further than many do go, but this thou mayest do, and yet be a Carnalist. Thou knowest this is the truth of God, and this stirs thine affections a little.

Thirdly, God may be, he hath quickened thy knowledge a little, and quickened thy conscience, and made it tell thee the horror of thy sins, and this may raise up thine affections many steps higher; not only to mourn for thy sins, and be full of the affections of sorrow, but also to go mournfully and sadly up and down, to pull down thy proud looks, to take on lamentably, because of thy former iniquities. As Ahab. Thus the word made Ahab rend the very clothes off his back, and fling off his royal robes, and put on sackcloth in their room, it made him have no mind to his meat, but to fast, yea, to go softly too, says the Text: 1 Kings 21:27. When Ahab heard these words, he tore off his clothes, he abstained from his meat, and went softly. Ambulabat demisso capite; that is, he did not go so proudly up and down with such a career in the streets, as before: No, he hung down his looks, he went sadly and softly up and down as he went. Thus far too thou mayest go in raising thine affections, and yet be a Carnalist. Thou mayest be smitten in thy soul for thy sins, as to go softly and sadly, and mournfully up and down, to have little lust to eat thy meat for thinking of thy sins, to go poorly and meanly, and have little mind to go bravely: I say, thine affections may be so quickened, as to go sadly all along as thou goest, so that all that knew thee before may wonder; good Lord, what ails yonder man, how is he changed? He was a Ruffian, a Royster, and who but he the other day? What's the matter with him? He goes so sadly up and down, and so pensively along. But why do I speak against thee, when there be few that are a quarter so well affected as thou? But alas, I tell thee, thou mayst go thus far, and be thus deeply affected, and yet be a Carnalist.

Fourthly, a deep apprehension and sense of the horror of thine estate: this may wind up thine affections many steps higher; thou mayst be afraid to be damned, and afraid of the judgments of God, and this may fetch tears from thine eyes, sighs and groans from thy heart. This may even melt thy affections into weepings, and abundance of weepings for the sins thou hast done, and yet be a Carnalist. The Prophet brings in the carnal Jews so doing, "This have you done again, covering the Altar of God with tears, with weeping and crying out; insomuch that he regardeth not the offering anymore." Mark, they offered their prayers unto God, and cried, and cried outright, yea, they poured out many tears, they covered God's Altar with tears, and yet says he, God regarded not their prayers and their offerings for all that: should we see a man come to God's house, and hear him at the hearing of the Word, or calling upon God, make an outcry of his sins, yea, weep and weep abundantly, cover his Pew with his tears, we would wonder at the repentance and the good affections of that man, yet so far thou mayst go, such good affections thou mayst have, as to cover thy Table with tears, yea, and God's Altar with thy weepings, and yet be a Carnalist. "Good men," says Homer, "are weeping men." Nay, I say a man may be a less weeping man, and yet be a good man. O how mightily may a man's affections be wrought on, and yet be a stranger from grace!

Fifthly, Self-love: look how high self-love may wind up thine affections for thy sins, so high may thine affections be wound up. Self-love may make thee wondrous affectionate. No natural affection can possibly be raised up higher than self-love may. Saint Paul, when reckoning up all the sinful affections of men in these last days, names self-love as foremost. "In the last days perilous times shall come," why? "For men shall be lovers of themselves": then he names eighteen more, but this he places in the front of the Catalogue, for self-love is strongest of all, 2 Timothy 3:2. I cite this text only to show how our affections may be raised to God, namely, as high as ever self-love can clamber. Self-love will make a man be very affectionate. When a man knows he cannot be saved unless he do thus and thus; O how affectionate may he be to do it, when he knows he shall perish forever if he be not religious and godly; if he do not bewail his iniquities and strive against sin, and labour to do good unto others: how marvellous full of affections may this make him to be, to do abundance of things!

First, It may screw up his affections so high, that he may be loath to commit sin: perhaps he often commits it, but he would gladly leave it. O he is unwilling to do it, he wishes affectionately, "O Lord, how shall I leave it? O that I might leave it": yea, he seeks some means to leave it; he does it, I confess, but fain would he not do it; his affections may be wrought upon thus far, and yet be a Carnalist. Such a one was Darius, he had made a Decree, and written it, and signed it, and sealed it. Well, Daniel would not do according to the tenor of the Decree: and therefore the Decree was, he should be cast into the Lions Den. The King did cast him in indeed, but lo, how unwilling he was to commit this sin: He fasted, he woke, he could not sleep a wink's sleep: He wished, "O that I might safely deliver him! O that thy God, O Daniel, would deliver thee." True, he thought "I must needs now do this sin; alas my Decree, and what may the Lord think of me? If I should not do it, all the Country would think me too blame, nay, they would rebel against me outright, for breaking the Laws of the Medes and the Persians. Alas! I must do it"; but it appears though, how unwilling he was to do it, he could neither eat, nor sleep, nor be merry, nor quiet, till he might hear Daniel was safe. Many a King but a quarter as great as he would have scorned to have troubled his thoughts about such a Puritan as Daniel was esteemed to be: nay, he rose early in the morning, before the time was expired, he ran in all post to the den of Lions, and there he cried lamentably, "O Daniel, thou servant of the living God: O Daniel," he screeched it out dolefully; and when he heard that Daniel was alive, he rejoiced exceedingly, Daniel 6:23. These subsequent circumstances show how unwilling he was in the punishment of committing the sin, if he could have helped it, and saved his honour with his Lords and his Nobles. Thus he was unwilling to commit the sin, yet a wretched man for all that. Men imagine they have a good Christian plea when they can say this for themselves; it's true, I do rap out an oath in my choler, I do pray coldly and with many by-thoughts, but God knows I am unwilling to do so, I would very fain have it otherwise; I am sorry I am drawn so away. Alas! So thou mayst be, and yet be a Carnalist: thou mayst pray, and be unwilling to pray carelessly, thou mayst repent in some manner, and be sorry thou repentest no more; thou mayst be loath to commit an offence, and yet be a mere natural man, no jot of saving grace in thee. Was not Pilate sensibly unwilling to condemn Jesus Christ? Was not Herod unwilling to behead John the Baptist? It spoiled all his mirth at his feast, that he was compelled to do it, for so he counted it a compulsion, otherwise he would not have done it: was not Saul unwilling to transgress the commandment of the Lord? He forced himself; he had abundance of gainsayings in his heart, abundance of wishes in his breast, "O I would not do it, I would to God I were not put upon such importunate circumstances as I am, fain would I not do it"; he forced himself, there was a kind of pitched field in his bosom, a battle in his soul: fain would he do it, that way went his lusts; fain would he not do it, that way went his conscience: So he forced himself, 1 Samuel 13:13. and yet God did reject him. Thus self-love may wind up a man's affections exceedingly, to be loath to commit a sin.

Secondly, It may so draw up one's affections to God as to make one vomit up a dear sin oneself and be sorry that others too should commit it; he may be vexed to see other men drunk, vexed to see them break the Sabbath, vexed to see how slack they come to God's house, vexed to hear anybody swear, or curse, or take on: he may be driven to make restitution himself. Thus it was with Micah, he had stolen eleven hundred Shekels of silver from his Mother; well, this man, as it appears, hears his Mother curse, swear, and take on, she had lost so much silver, somebody had stolen it from her; when he heard his Mother curse and ban in this fashion, he was so deeply moved to hear it, that he could not abide it: nay, it made him be willing to confess he had stolen it from her, and to make restitution of all, yea, so far as his mother did think, O what a blessed convert was her son! He was now converted to be of so honest a mind. "Blessed be thou of the Lord my son," says his Mother. He said unto his Mother, "The eleven hundred shekels of silver that were taken from thee, about which thou cursedst, and spakest of also in mine ears, behold, the silver is with me, I took it": and his Mother said, "Blessed be thou of the Lord, my son," Judges 17:2. He had stolen the silver from his Mother, and yet when he heard his Mother curse and swear in that manner, it should seem his affections did burn him. What, shall I hear my Mother curse in this sort? And rather than he would let her stand swearing and cursing, he would vomit up his sweet earnings. Nay, she thought him so religious as passes because he did so. "Blessed be thou of the Lord, my son": but she was deceived, for he was a wretched Idolater; the Lord calls him an Idolater, verse 5. Beloved, this is a strange thing indeed; yet thus far may a Carnalist go: he may be zealous against other men's sins, and grieved to hear others transgress, and vexed to see others offend. When David would sin and number the people, it vexed the soul of Joab to see it. "O my Lord the King, why wilt thou be a cause of trespass to Israel?" 1

Chronicles 21:3. So thou mayst be vexed to see others offended, and yet notwithstanding no better than a Carnalist.

Thirdly, It may so raise up his affections to God, and to be so set against sin, as to be willing to lose hopes of getting housefuls of silver and gold, to lose the favour of Kings and of Princes, to lose preferment and all, than venture on a sin. This was Balaam's case, "If Balak would give me his house full of silver and gold, I cannot go beyond the commandment of God to do less or more," Numbers 24:13. He dared not go beyond the commandment of God a jot, no, not for a house full of money, which is more than a thousand can say, that will go beyond it, and beside it, and against the commandment of God for a handful of Barley; yet he though a Reprobate, dared not go beyond the commandment of God to do good or bad of his own mind, not for a house full of coin. "Knowest thou not," says King Balak unto him, "knowest thou not that I can promote thee to honour?" yea, he knew it well enough, and yet for all that Balaam would not yield to him. Balaam, if he would have hearkened to carnal arguments, he might have found many. "The Israelites are a people of another Nation. I am a Moabite, and they are of another generation: and what though they be better people then they, yet I am a Subject to the King of Moab, and I must be true to my Sovereign, and count them mine enemies which are the enemies of my Country, and are come to lick up the land. If I do obey my King, I may have money by housefuls, I may have preferment as much and more then I can wish." Thus flesh and blood might have reasoned; but see how his affections were better rectified than thus; he dared not do it upon any terms because it was against the commandment of God. "Thou thinkest thy cause to be happy, O thou canst be willing to pass by the wages of sin, though thou couldest get by a sin, yet thou darest not commit it: thou thinkest certainly mine affections are to God and to grace. I might get this, and

I might get that, if I would but go against my conscience a little, but I will not for money, nor favour, nor anything." Well said yet; better than millions can say: but this thou mayst do, and yet be a Carnalist.

Fourthly, It may elevate his affections so high as to be so forward in religion and godliness: so strict in his ways, as to be persecuted too for the truth's sake, and for Christ's sake: he may endure persecution for a good while: indeed, if it goes too far, he will warp: but persecuted he may be, and suffer for a good while he may, and yet be a carnal man. This you may see in the stony-ground hearer, "He hears the Word and receives it with joy," Matthew 13:20. Mark, his affections are raised, he receives the Word and the Gospel with joy, he is affected with the Word, nay, says our Saviour, "he endures for a while, and persecution arises against him, then he is offended," verse 21. It's true, he is offended at this, that he should suffer persecution; he would be glad to be a professor of the Word, so he might profess it in a whole skin, as we say: he does, and he will warp then, that's certain: that's all one; nevertheless, you may observe in the meantime what a great way he goes in religion, he trades so far in it, that others will persecute him for it, and yet but a carnal man for all that. Now of the good ground.

Fifthly, It may lift up his affections so high as to ravish him and enamour him with joys of the Spirit. He may be in some ecstasies of spiritual joy: as many examples might be named. Were not the Galatians enamoured with the Gospel that would have plucked out their eyes and given them to Paul? Were not the people overjoyed when they cried out in the open Congregation, "Lord, evermore give us this bread"? Oh then, set your affections, etc.

THE THIRD SERMON.

"Set your affections on things that are above, and not on things which are on the earth." – Colossians 3:2

The last thing that I told you was what a great way a carnal man may go in this point. His affections may be wrought on exceedingly. I promised to show you that this was no argument that his affections are set upon God. The Apostle does not say, let the things that are above work on your affections, for so they may do, and ye be carnal for all that; but he says, "Set your affections on things which are above."

There are four reasons to prove, though a carnal man's affections be so wrought on as you have heard, that they are not rightly wrought on.

First, Because they are not kindly wrought on. They are chafed and heated very much, but they are not kindly wrought on. The affections must be kindly wrought on, otherwise they are not wrought on aright; they may be violently and passionately wrought on, there may be a great deal of pother wrought in the affections, but never are they rightly wrought on, unless they be wrought upon kindly. "Be kindly affectioned one to another with brotherly love," says St. Paul, Romans 12:10. The

Galatians that would have plucked out their eyes for Saint Paul, they were strongly affected with Saint Paul, but they were not kindly affected. If they had been kindly affected with him or his Doctrine, they would not have hearkened to false Apostles, as they did. A carnal man, natural reason, and knowledge out of the Word may work on his affections, his conscience, and self-love, whereby he is loath to be damned, and glad to be saved when he dies, these may work on his affections, and cause him to weep for his sins, and give over many corruptions, and to be strongly affected, but alas he is not kindly affected. It's only the love of God shed abroad in the heart that kindly affects one. But it's self-love, and not love of the Lord Jesus that affects him: he is not kindly affected.

Secondly, A carnal man's affections are not judiciously wrought on. They are wrought on in a fit at it, but they are not wrought on with judgment, they have not the true beginning of working, which is sound judgment. St. Jerome says of the affections of Christ, respectu Christi semper sequuntur rationem, Christ's affections had always the right beginning, which was true reason and judgment. And therefore St. Matthew notes especially the beginning of his sorrow, "He began to be sorrowful and very heavy," Matthew 26:37. He had a right beginning of it. The natural beginning of the affections is this, when the judgment is first poised, and the heart is first fired, this is the natural beginning of the affections. So that the heart must first be wrought on, and the spirit moved, before the affections can be judiciously wrought on. And therefore says St. John, Christ troubled himself. He groaned in spirit, and he troubled himself, John 11:33. He was exceedingly affected with sorrow for Lazarus his death, and his kinsfolk's sorrows and distrusts they were in, and he troubled himself: we translate it, he was troubled, but in the original it is, ἐνεβριμήσατο τῷ πνεύματι, he troubled himself, his own judgment, and his spirit, and his heart stirred up his affections to be troubled. His affections were wrought on judiciously. A carnal man's affections though they be much wrought on, yet they are not wrought on judiciously. Now he is in the mind to be strict and to be godly, now he weeps and takes on, can you wonder? His conscience now jerks him, and is quick: but when a few tears and a few labours and endeavours that way have contented his conscience, as his conscience is apt to be satisfied, the man is of another judgment then quickly. He is of the judgment then, tush, what need I be so strict and precise? Thus he is affected, not upon sound judgment. Affected he is, and strongly affected too for the while, but he is not affected judiciously.

Thirdly, A carnal man's affections are not wrought upon regularly. His affections are wrought upon by God's justice and judgments because God is a consuming fire against sin, because God is severe against the works of iniquity, because he has made heaven-gate to be straight. These are the grounds of his work. His affections are wrought upon this way; therefore, he weeps, and therefore he prays, and therefore he reforms, and therefore he is affected. But this is not regular affection: he is affected with fear, but it is not the fear of God's goodness, not God's mercy and goodness, were there no other attribute in God, he might look long enough before he would fear his mercy: that's a ground of presumption to him, but he fears God's judgments and his justice; he does not tremble and quake to consider that God is a merciful God, and a good God whom he has sinned against. The true Israel of God, "They fear the Lord and his goodness," Hos. 3:5. Their affections are regular, they are affected with fear of God's goodness. But a carnal man is not affected with the fear of God's goodness. He is affected with the fear of God's justice, his affections are wrought on irregularly.

Fourthly, A carnal man's affections are not wrought upon universally. Some affections are wrought on, and others are not. No, he has a contradiction of affections. He has some good affections to God and to grace, and he has some affections that are contradictory to these. Some sins he grieves under, some he is glad under; some commandments he delights to be doing, and some he delights to be breaking. I do not mean part flesh, and part spirit, for so the best godly souls under Heaven have a contradiction of affections: they have some affections of the spirit, and some affections of the flesh, contradicting and opposing one another. I do not mean this. But a carnal man has such a contradiction of affections, as that his carnal affections give the other the lie. He is affected with sorrow for his sins, but he is not troubled for his usury. He is affected with desires to leave his sins, but not to leave his sinful dependencies. As Esau, he was affected with weeping for his missing of grace and the blessing, but not for his pleasures and sensual delight. Is not this a contradiction of affections! He found no place of repentance, though he sought it carefully with tears, Heb. 12:17. He was affected with weeping after repentance, but he could find no place to bestow it in. There was not elbow-room enough for repentance in his heart. He made some room in some part of his heart for repentance, but not in all. He found a place for it in some of his affections, but not in all. He is affected, but he is not affected universally. He has a contradiction of affections in his soul; so that a carnal man's affections, though they be wrought on, they are not wrought upon universally.

It is true, a carnal man's affections may be exceedingly wrought on, then I pray examine yourselves; Two persons I would have to examine themselves:

First, those who think their affections are set upon God. As for those who are absolutely carnal, whose affections are buried in the things of the world, and have no affection at all unto grace or holiness, speak not to them; their own consciences condemn them to be rotten and are as good as a thousand examiners. I do not speak to them. If they will not hear their own consciences, much less will they hear me. I speak to those who think their affections are set upon God.

Secondly, those who, though their affections may be set upon Christ, yet think they are not affected aright; for many Christian souls are rightly affected and do not think so. Examine yourselves whether you are rightly affected or not.

First, He who is truly affected with grace and with Christ and his Word, he affects nothing so much as he does grace. A carnal man may be greatly affected with grace, but there is something he affects more. He affects his vanities more, and his profits more, and his pleasures more. Herod, it is true, he affected John the Baptist, he knew he was a just man, and he feared him: he affected his preaching, for he heard him gladly, he affected the practice of his doctrine, for he did many things; he was affected greatly with these good things, but there was something he was affected with more. The daughter of Herodias affected him more. She pleased Herod, says the text, Mark 6:22. He was not only affected with her dancing but affected to content. She pleased Herod. John the Baptist did not please him; he had not content in his ministry. Nay, her dancing affected him so much that he was willing to part with half of his kingdom to gratify her. "Whatever you shall ask of me," says he, "I will give it you, to the half of my kingdom." This was more affection than ever he showed to John's doctrine. He never said to John or his doctrine, "I will part with a quarter of my kingdom;" nay, he would not part with his whore nor his lusts for that. Nay, he would rather see John dead, as well as he affected him, than miss of his pleasures or not gratify his lords. "I will give you," says he to his damsel, "I will give you half of my kingdom." "Give me then," says she, "John Baptist's head in a charger." The foolish king had not wit enough to say, "John is dearer than all my kingdom."

No, he affected his teaching well, but his pastime better. Examine your soul by this mark: you are affected with grace, but is there nothing you are affected with more? You are glad to hear a sermon, but may we not see you gladder at your sports? You are glad to part with an hour at God's worship, but are you not gladder to part with two at your profits? A child of God is affected with grace most; let credit fly, let profit fly, let carnal relations fly, let life, let living, let all that he has fly, rather than let a good duty of grace fly away; he is most affected with grace; there is nothing he affects more or so much.

Secondly, he who is affected with grace and godliness aright must needs have expressions of grace; he cannot but show it; he can as easily carry fire in his bosom and hide it as conceal grace. Can a man be deeply affected with sorrows and not show it in his face; can a man be deeply affected with passions of anger and of wrath and not show it in his countenance? Hands, feet, lips, nostrils, eyes, forehead—yea, and all a man's gestures and carriage will show what affections are in him. Affectio taciturna nulla est affectio. Every passion has its proper dialect. Concealed affection is no affection at all, or but small and as good as nothing. So if you are affected with grace, it will show itself in your speeches, in your actions, in your ways; it will show itself in your calling; it will show itself in your company; it will show itself at the table; it will show itself in the market; you cannot be affected with grace but you will be an open professor of grace. Can a man take fire in his bosom, and his clothes not be burnt? (Proverbs 6:27). If fire be in your bosom, all who come near you will feel the very smell of it in your clothes. The affections are a fire. "The fire kindled," says David (Psalm 39:3), that is, his affections did kindle; he strove to hide them, but he could not; can you not be religious but you must show it? Says the mocker of all goodness. No, it is a sign you have no affection to holiness, because you will not show it: you can hear

God dishonoured with oaths and not show your affection against them; you can come in company and suffer unprofitable language and not show your affections to holy discourse; a sign you have no affections that way; you may say you are affected with grace, but how does it appear? It appears not in your prayers, little or no affection in them; it appears not in the Sabbath, little or no attention to the sanctifying of it. Like the stupid fool in the comedy, who, being willing to be thought to be angry, he knew not how to show it, but only by saying, Irascor, "I am angry," says he; one would think if he were angry, he needed not to say he was angry; the affection of anger would have expressed itself, but he had no other reasons to be thought to be angry but only his saying, "I am angry." So you have no other expressions of affection at the word or at grace, but only you say, "I am affected therewith." Concealed affection is no affection. De non apparentibus et de non existentibus eadem est ratio, it's a good rule in law. There is the same reason for things which appear not, that is for things which exist not. Certainly here it is most true, I may be confident to say, if your affections appear not, your affections are not.

Thirdly, he who is affected with grace or holiness, if he be even slightly interrupted, he is troubled; it's like the stopping of a watercourse, the water swells and is troubled exceedingly that it cannot pass; like the Woman in the Gospel, whose affections were for Christ to anoint his head; when his disciples cast a rub in her way, saying it would have been better bestowed on the poor, "Why trouble ye the woman?" says Christ (Matthew 26:10). Christ knew it troubled her affections to be hindered from their course; he who is truly affected with Christ or his Spirit, if he does not find Christ sooner, he is sick with love. "I charge you, O ye daughters of Jerusalem, if ye find my beloved, that ye tell him I am sick with love," (Song of Solomon 5:8). Her poor soul was even sick at heart for her love because she could not reach him: examine yourself in this point. I am sure you have been long enough without Christ; you are 20 or 30 years old, and all this while you have been without Christ: you say you are affected with Christ, oh, you would love to have Christ; you would love to have him dwell in you forever; answer me now, are you sick with love for Christ? Hope deferred makes the heart sick (Proverbs 13:12). You say you are affected with hopes after grace, you hope for grace and for strength against sin, but your hope is deferred, it has not come yet; you are not able to withstand your corruptions, not able to subdue such a lust; no, if you are affected at all with any hope, your hope is deferred as yet: but has it made your heart sick? Were you ever sick at heart for this grace? If it has not made your heart sick, it is a sign you were never rightly affected with hope, for if you were, it would make your heart sick to be so long without it, as you have been. Perhaps your affections are so strongly set on the world that you have been world-sick, and cross-sick, and trouble-sick, and anger-sick, and revenge-sick, and covetousness-sick; as Ahab was sick because he knew not how to get Naboth's vineyard (1 Kings 21:4). Maybe you are crossed and sick with vexation; perhaps you are incensed and sick with revenge or impatience: but are you sick for grace? Aristotle calls the affections Aegritudines animi, they are the sicknesses of the soul; if the soul is truly affected, she is sick if she does not succeed.

Fourthly, he who is truly affected with grace has his conversation in heaven, from where all grace descends. Animus est non ubi animat, sed ubi amat, the soul is not where it animates, not where it sojourns, but where it affects; and therefore you live in heaven if you are truly affected with heavenly things: he who is truly affected with grace is most affected with the fountain of grace, which is God. God is the fountain of all grace, and if you are affected with it, you are chiefly affected with God. Alas! You may have a good memory, a good wit, and good parts, and be affected with them, and rejoice that you have them. But the question is this, are you affected with God, the fountain of grace? A wicked man may be affected with grace in the bucket, and yet have no love for grace in the fountain: it affects him well enough to have some, but he does not like it to have much, Omne nimium vertitur in nigrum monachum, thinks he. It is the property of the godly to be affected with God. "Rejoice in the Lord, O ye righteous," (Psalm 33:1). Be affected with God himself, says the Psalmist. One is affected with pleasures, another with honour and respect, another with profit; another may be affected with grace too, but it is the godly man only who is affected with God himself. Examine your affections, are you affected with God himself? Are you affected with his glory?

It is infinitely important for us to have our affections set right; which I will prove by these 8 arguments.

Firstly, hereby only are we marriageable to Christ. When a man goes wooing for a wife, all his care is to get her affections; he will never marry her if he is wise, if he may not have her affection. "The affections are the womanhood of the soul," says Philo. He will never marry her if she is not a woman for him; much less will he marry her if she is not a woman at all. She is not marriageable but only for her affection; what a miserable soul then is your soul if your affections are not right? You are not marriageable to Christ. This is the rule of all wives and of all spouses, "thy desire shall be to thy husband," (Genesis 3:16). Your affections shall be to him, or you cannot be his wife. He is a monster in nature who will have a wife whose affection is set on another. Do you take Christ for a monster, that your soul should be married to him when your affection is elsewhere? If your affections are to the world and to worldly things, Christ cannot abide you. Do you not know that the love of the world is enmity with God? O you filthy soul, betrothing your affections to the world and yet hoping to be married to Christ? You are not marriageable to him. If gains, pleasures, vanities, and such base paramours are welcomed to your heart, you cannot be married unto Christ; you are the world's spouse and the devil's spouse when your affections are inordinate. "Uncleanness and inordinate affection," the apostle puts them together, "mortify your members which are on the earth, fornication, uncleanness, inordinate affection," (Colossians 3:5). So your soul is a filthy and an unclean soul that has these inordinate affections unmortified in you. Your soul is a fit spouse for the unclean spirit, and not for Christ, and therefore, it deeply concerns you to have your affections set right, because thereby only are you marriageable to Christ.

Secondly, hereby only does the soul set up favourites in her heart: those are the heart's favourites whom the heart most affects. If Christ is not your heart's favourite, what a woeful condition are you in? It has been the undoing of many a prince, the having of ill favourites; and that soul must necessarily be forever undone that has ill favourites in her heart. As soon as Joseph was in favour with the keeper of the prison, Joseph had all at command; nothing was done but Joseph was the doer of it, (Genesis 39:21). He was no sooner in favour but he ruled all. Look what your heart does affect, that is in favour with your heart; that is dominus fac totum. If your pleasures and your vanities are once in favour with your heart, Christ can have no command of your heart, no further than your lusts will give leave. You cannot reform anything that is amiss, no further than your lusts will give leave. Would you repent, or stand for God's glory? You cannot unless your lusts do give leave. Would you be reproved, or well counselled? You cannot unless your lusts will give leave. As long as your lusts are in favour with your heart, they govern all, they command all, your mind goes as they tend, your thoughts come as they call, your courses are as they will. "I will give this people favour in the sight of the Egyptians, and they shall spoil the Egyptians," (Exodus 3:21-22). When they were once in favour with them, they might spoil them, rob them, and borrow jewels from them, and never pay them back; they might do anything when they were in favour with them. Oh, the misery of the soul when the world, or pleasure, or sin, or the like are in favour with it! They spoil it, rob it, and bereave it of all the jewels it has. Christ can do nothing to any purpose with that soul that favours other things besides Christ. Now, if your affections are not set right, your favour is not right set. This is the reason why you are wedded to the world and wedded to your lusts, that your affections cannot be unto Christ. When Hadad had great favour with Pharaoh, Pharaoh even married his own wife's sister unto Hadad, (1 Kings 11:19). He made him his brother, brought him into the nearest relation he could, when his favour was set towards him. So if you favour the things of this life, you wed your soul to them. What an infinite indignity is this unto Christ, that such base and sordid things should be in favour, and Christ not be your soul's favourite!

Thirdly, hereby the soul is convertible and reconcilable to God. However cross and crooked a man may be, however cruelly and implacably bent to transgress, as long as there are affections in him to be wrought, his heart may be won. Though a king's wrath be as the roaring of a lion, though he may be fallen out with a man, as long as there are affections in the king, patience, wisdom, humbling oneself, and the like, these things may persuade him. "By long forbearing is a prince persuaded," (Proverbs 15:15). Without a man has any affections in him, he is not capable of persuasion, says Aristotle. The affections are what make a man mutable. Though it be a weakness to be mutable, yet when a man is evil and wicked, it's a blessed weakness that he is mutable from that wickedness. Now, if a man is grievously set upon mischief, though he be an enemy of all grace and goodness, as long as there are any affections left in him, he is not an implacable enemy. No, his affections are a possible subject to be wrought on; the Word and the Spirit may persuade him. Therefore, what care should we have of our affections, because thereby we are placable and reconcilable to God? The apostle yokes these two together, "without natural affection, implacable," (Romans 1:31). As long as a man has any natural affection left, he is never implacable; still, he may be persuaded, unless he degenerates in his affections and proves to be unnatural. If the affections degenerate in this fashion, he is not only wicked and an enemy to grace, but he is an implacable enemy. Think then what wrong you do to your own souls, so unnaturally to set your affections, to let them degenerate as you do, and wander after vanity. Beware how you do so; you go about to divert all possibility of conversion and provoke the Lord to count you implacable enemies to grace and to the sceptre of his dear Son.

Fourthly, it may appear how infinitely it stands you in hand to set your affections aright, because the affections are the hands of your souls. You cannot take hold of anything in the world to do you any good, but by your affections. For as hands are to the body, so the affections are to the soul. Will a man be so mad as to put his hand and his fingers out of joint? Alas! He cannot take hold of so much as his food to eat it. So the affections are the hands of the soul. "He that hath clean hands and a pure heart," (Psalms 24:4), that is, he whose affections are clean and heart pure. "I will wash my hands in innocence, and so will I compass thine altar," (Psalms 26:6), that is, I will purge my affections, and so I will pray. "I will that men pray everywhere, lifting up holy hands without wrath," (1 Timothy 2:8), that is, lifting up holy affections, without the distempered affections of wrath or anger or the like. The affections are the hands of the heart, whereby it takes the word or the commandment or anything to it. Now, what a horrible thing is it that these hands of yours should be put out of joint? As long as your affections are to the things here on earth, they are all out of joint; you can never take hold of grace. You cannot take hold of a promise or of the word unless your affections are right. I know that faith is the right hand of the soul, whereby it takes hold of that which is good. But alas! The hand of faith is clumsy without the affections. When someone has a cross, how do they take it? That is, how are they affected under it? You take it ill to be reproved of your sins; you take it ill to be warned and admonished either in public or private. You take it ill to be told of the judgments of God against your lusts. Alas! How can you do otherwise? You cannot take it well when your affections, which should take it well, are set upon vanity. Will you bind up and hamper your affections in the things of the earth? Alas! Your hands are quite bound; you cannot take hold of Christ or of heaven. You even pinion your own soul and shackle it for hell. What does the devil do when he shackles a man like a prisoner for hell and damnation? He binds him hand and foot and casts him into utter darkness; he binds up his heart and affections so that he cannot weep, he cannot repent of his sins, he cannot rejoice in grace or in goodness, he cannot delight in the word. He binds up his affections, which are the hands and feet of the soul, and so fits him for hell and destruction. Above all things then, be sure that your hands be loose and your affections at liberty to set them upon heaven.

Fifthly, it may appear how infinitely it stands you in hand to set your affections aright, because they are not only the hands, but the handles of your hearts. As your hearts can catch hold of nothing that is good unless your affections take hold, so nothing can take hold of your hearts but by your affections. If ever the word does convert you, it must catch hold of you. "Jesus said unto Simon, henceforth thou shalt catch men," (Luke 5:10), that is, the preaching of the word, it shall catch men when you preach. Now, one of the first holds that it catches is by the affections. Men are affected with the word, and so it comes to convert men. Now beloved, have you not need to have a care of affections, seeing they are the handles of your hearts? Were it not for them, the word could never catch hold on you. There is no hold to be had of such a man, as we say; that is, his affections are slippery. Beloved, here you come to God's house, miserable wretched souls, in your sins. Alas! How is it possible that ever God's ministers should catch hold of your hearts? Your affections are the main hold that we can catch of you. If your affections are not here but run after the things of this life, we can have no hold of you; you have nothing that we should take hold by. Indeed, we may catch hold of your understandings; that's nothing unless we take hold of your affections. They are as slippery eels; we can scarce ever hold them. O could we take hold of them, it were well; they are fair handles for us to take hold by. O if we could but truly affect your hearts with the truth, then we might have some hope to convert you. As Epictetus says of wrongs and of injuries and all things in the world, "everything hath two handles." O says he, "if a man could take hold of every wrong at the right handle, then he would bear it patiently." So I may say of your hearts. Your hearts have two handles. I pray God the word may take hold at the right handle of your hearts. The true affections of the heart, if ever the word takes hold of them, it has taken hold of the right handle. Is it not then a lamentable thing that men's affections are misplaced? Alas! They are the hold of the heart, and the heart can never be taken unless they be set right.

Sixthly, it may appear how infinitely it stands you in hand to set your affections aright, because they are the soul's stomach: that which the soul does affect, that feeds and fills the soul, as food does the stomach. Is it not necessary to be careful what food we eat? If we eat trash, it will kill us; if we feed upon poison, it will poison and infect us. Now, that is the food of your soul, which your soul does affect, and your affection is your soul's stomach to hunger after it; your affections are the appetite of the soul. Such then as your affections are, such is your food. Should you see a man feed upon dirt, bricks, and carrion, certainly you would say, unless he is broken therefrom, it will kill him. No remedy but it will kill him without doubt. And will you feed your soul with vanities, trash, and poison? Everything is trash besides Christ; everything is poison besides Christ and his graces. If you feed upon anything besides Christ and his spirit, you feed upon trash and poison. Now, if you set your affections here below, you feed upon trash. You murder your soul with such food; it's rank poison, and yet you feed upon it. That which you affect, that's your soul's food. "As newborn babes desire the sincere milk of the Word, that you may grow thereby," (1 Peter 2:2). Milk, you know, is the babe's food; if it does not have its food, it cannot possibly live. But the word is the milk and the food of the soul, and that the apostle would have you to set your affections upon. Desire it, or affect it, says he; where note your affections are the stomach of your soul. The Word is your food. All other food is but trash, and it feeds you accordingly. O you poor souls that feed upon poison all the day long, that diet your souls with nothing but trash, filth, and froth, how long will you do thus? O set your affections on things that are above; these are the wholesome food of your souls, etc.

Seventhly, it may appear how infinitely it stands you in hand to set your affections aright, because they are the main matter of grace. They are the materials of grace: as Aristotle says of the virtues, they are nothing but the right ruling of the affections, so may I say of grace with a little alteration, the main work of grace is the ruling of the affections aright. It takes them off from the things here on earth and lifts them up to the things that are in heaven. When grace does convert a man, it does not take away the affections, but it rules them. You were angry before; grace does not take away your anger. No, "a good man must be angry," says Cicero. I say grace does not take away your anger, but it rules your anger and teaches you to turn it against sin and against the dishonour of God. You were merrily disposed before, of a cheerful constitution; grace does not come to take away your mirth, but to rule it. Whereas you were merry with vanity, and ever laughing at jests and at fooleries, now grace makes you merry in God's service and to rejoice in the Lord. You were of a sad spirit before, but perhaps it was for crosses, losses, discontents, and the like. Grace comes not to take away your sorrows, but to rule them, to make you weep and mourn at your deadness and unthankfulness toward the Lord Jesus Christ.

Gratia non tollit, sed attollit naturam. Grace does not take away nature, but it elevates it. The affections are natural; grace turns them into spiritual. This, I say brethren, so that you may see how grace runs along in the affections, as water in a pipe. The affections are the matter of grace. As the soul is in the body, the body is the matter, and the soul is in it, making up a living creature. A man needs to look after his body, for it is the due matter of his soul; so it is with the affections. You need to be careful of them, for they are the matter of grace. Therefore, the Apostle calls the affections the members: "yield your members servants unto righteousness" (Romans 6:19), which, as exposited, refers to yielding your affections thereto.

For they are your soul's members and the materials of grace. Is not fear the matter of the fear of the Lord? And love the matter of the love of the Lord? And sorrow the matter of repentance from sin? Now, if the affections are the materials of grace, what a desperate condition you are in when you set your affections upon earthly things! You throw down all the material for grace. How can you have any grace when you cast away in the kennel all the matter for grace? Grace requires the affections for its material, and you have no material for this grace. You hurl away all your affections upon your pleasures, profits, and vanities. You are so far from all grace that you have no material for grace.

Eighthly, it may appear how infinitely it stands you in hand to set your affections aright because they are arguments for what you are. According to your affections, so are your souls. If I could see what your affections run on, I could see what you all are: whether saints or wicked, whether of God or the Devil. The affections are the arguments that a man is a man. When the people of Lystra took Paul and Barnabas for gods and wanted to sacrifice to them, Paul said, "Sirs, why do you do this? We are men of like passions with you" (Acts 14:15), meaning affections: we have fear, joy, grief, love, and similar passions with you. Now, if the mere possession of affections is the argument that a man is a man, then surely the goodness or vanity of these affections is the argument that a man is a Christian man or an ungodly man. I beseech you to consider what a woeful, distressed condition you are in if your affections are vain and earthly. You carry a brand in your hearts that you are not of God, that you are still the slaves of Satan and the servants of unrighteousness, and your end is no better than eternal death and destruction. "Affectus virum indicat." Your affections show you what men and women you are, etc.

THE FOURTH SERMON.

"Set your affections on things that are above, and not on things which are on the earth." – Colossians 3:2

Hitherto it suffices to have spoken of the coherence of the words, wherein you have heard:

First, what these affections are.

Secondly, that a wicked man cannot set his affections on God.

Thirdly, how far a wicked man may have good affections, and how they differ from the godly's.

Fourthly, how they may examine themselves and find that their affections are not set right.

Fifthly, eight several arguments to convince them what a woeful condition they are in until their affections are set upon God.

Now for the words, they contain a special duty that a Christian is bound to, namely, to set his affections upon God. The Apostle presses it strongly.

Firstly, because it is an infallible mark of our being or not being in Christ. "If you be risen with Christ, etc., set your affections on things above." As if he should say, "You say you are risen with Christ, then demonstrate it now that you are risen with Christ. If you are risen with Christ, this will infallibly follow. You will set your affections above; it cannot be otherwise. If your affections are not set above, doubtless you are not risen with Christ." "Those that are Christ's," says Saint Paul, "have crucified the flesh with the affections and lusts," Galatians 5:24. He takes it for granted that if they are Christ's, they have crucified the flesh and the affections towards the world and set them upon God.

Secondly, he presses it as a matter of reasonable equity; the competition stands but between two, either things in heaven or things on earth. One of them you must set your affections upon; you cannot set your affections upon both. If you set your affections anywhere, you must needs set them upon one of these two. Mark the competition. "Set your affections on things that are above, not on the things on the earth." Now there is a necessity of reason that election should be made of the best, that we should set our affections on the better of the twain; to wit, the things that are in heaven, which are infinitely better than the things here on earth. "Set your affections on things that are above, and not on the things on earth." So hence you may see the necessity of this duty. We must set our affections above, or, which is all one, upon God. The strength of this necessity will the better appear if we consider these four things.

Firstly, that God is the principal object of our affections: as the eye is made to be set upon colours, and the ear is made to be set upon sounds, and the smell is made to be set upon odours; so the affections are made to be principally set upon God. The affections are so naturally due unto God that if it is not God the soul's affections are set on, it makes it a god or an idol. And therefore the Apostle bids us mortify our inordinate affections, evil concupiscence, and covetousness, which is idolatry, Colossians 3:5. When our affections are set upon gains, and upon profits, and the things of this life, the Apostle calls this covetousness, and this covetousness he says is idolatry; because the soul makes gold a god, and silver a god, and profit a god, by setting its affections thereupon. As the eye does either see colours, or else it sees a thing under the likeness of a colour: colour is the principal object of the sight, and therefore if it is not a colour which it sees (as the eye may see light, as the light of the fire, the light of the sun, but it sees it under the likeness of redness or whiteness, or some other colour.) It appears by a colour, or else it cannot see it: so beloved, it is either God our affections are on, or we idolize it as a god. Indeed, we may affect other things as mediums and in reference to God, but look where we set our affections, that is our god. "Only fear the Lord, and serve him with all your heart," 1 Samuel 12:24. We must set our affection of fear only upon God. The affections are the soul's attendants. Does not a servant wait only upon his own master? Whom he gives his attendance unto him he makes his master, and whom should the soul wait on but only upon God? The affections are the soul's attendants; upon whomever she bestows them, she waits upon it as the true God. "My soul," says David, "wait thou only upon God," Psalm 62:5. Give thine attendance to none but to him. Thine affections of love, and of joy, and of hope and desire, these must wait upon God for to worship him. Thine affections of fear and of care, these must wait upon God to provide whatever may please him. Thine affections of hatred, and of grief, and sorrow, and the like, these must wait as a guard to keep off whatever may offend him; thine affections are principally for God; this is the first ground, the affections were made for God.

Secondly, as the affections were principally made for this purpose, to be set upon God, so nothing but God has that which the affections look for. It is God whom the affections look for, and where can the affections find it but only in God? "There is none good but one, that is God," Matthew 19:17. The young man would have thought he sought for good in a right place when he sought for it in Christ. But as Chrysostom observes, "When he looked upon Christ as a mere man, Christ tells him he was mistaken in calling him good, there is none good but one, that is God." Christ himself, as near as he was unto good, as he came nearer to it than any creature in heaven or on earth, yet if he had been a creature, and men had set their affections on him as their good, being a creature, they had set their affections amiss: "Why callest thou me good?" says he; so much more does every creature answer, "Thou thinkest riches, honours, and pleasures are good. Why call ye me good?" may they all say, "there's none good but one, that is God." Will a man seek for the sun in a pail of water? Indeed, if the sun shines on the water, there you may see it. But if the sun does not look on it, you may look over all the waters in the world, and never find the sun in them all. So will you set your affections on the things of the world? It is good your affections look for, can you find any good in these things? Alas! Alas! Thou mayst have all the things of this world, yet if God does not show thee his face and his grace in the same, "stultus ad cribrum," thou runnest to them as a fool to a sieve. The sieve seems to hold a great deal of water, but by pulling the sieve from the water, the fool lost all the water. So riches, wealth, and pleasures, as long as thou hast them in grace and in God, they are like sieves in the water, full of water as long as they are in. So these are full of good, as long as they are in God and in grace; but if thou dost not set thine affections upon God, thine affections are befooled, and therefore thou must set thine affections upon God, because nothing but God has that which thine affections look for. It is good which the affections look for, and thine affections can find it nowhere but in God.

Thirdly, as nothing but God has that which the affections look for, nothing is good but he, so nothing is my good but only he, for if it be good, and not my good, this discontents mine affections; mine affections look at my good. I know compassion, and mercy, and love may look at the good of another; but then they consider some kind of propriety in that other, either as my brother, or friend, or my neighbour, still the affections have an eye unto my good, thine affections to thy good. Now nothing in the world can so truly be said thy good as thy God. Other goods are called this world's goods, 1 John 3:17. They are the goods of this world rather than thy goods: but God is thy goodness: "Thou art my goodness, O Lord," says the Psalmist, Psalm 144:2. Thou canst not say of thy pleasures, "this is my goodness," nor of wealth, "this is my goodness"; nor of anything in the world, "this is my goodness": the good that is in it is the goodness of the thing, not thy goodness; if I should say, "this is thy goodness," it's all one as if I should say, thou hast no goodness, for that is none of thine, but only by possession, it is not thy goodness. And therefore how canst thou set thine affections upon it?

Firstly, it is only the good of thy body; it is not thy good. "Anima hominis est homo," says Plato. The soul is the man rather than the body. If the things of this life are the goods of the body, then how canst thou set thine affections upon them? Thine affections are the affections of thy soul. Meat is good; let thy body hunger after it, and thou sinnest not. Drink is good; let thy body thirst after it, thou errest not. But wilt thou set thine affections upon it? When it is not thy good, but only the good of thy body, it is not thy good. Means and maintenance are the good of thy body; house, lands, and livings, these are the good of thy body. Let the desires of thy body be to them; this is well yet. But if the desires of thy soul be thereto, if thou set thine affections upon them, thou art a beast, because they are not thy good. As Theophylact well observes upon the rich man in the Gospel, "Soul, thou hast much goods laid up for many years," Luke 12:19. "Take thine ease, eat, drink, and be merry." See the baseness of this fool's affections, says Theophylact: to eat, to drink, and to be merry; these were the goods of his unreasonable part. To rejoice in God's Law, to rejoice in holy thoughts and meditations, these are the goods of the soul, of the reasonable soul of a man. Now the fool he had none of these goods laid up; and yet he says, "Soul, thou hast much good laid up for many years," whereas that very night he died and was damned forever. The things of this life then are not thy good, and therefore thou must not set thine affections upon them.

Secondly, it is not thy good because it is not as long as thou art. Thou must live forever in heaven or in hell. Now all the goods of this life last but this life, and when thou diest, thou must leave them to others, and therefore they are not thy goods. Were they thy goods, thou mightest carry them away with thee when thou diest; but this cannot be. Canst thou carry thy barns and thy houses to heaven or to hell with thee? Canst thou carry thy dogs and thy hounds, and thy pleasures, and thy preferments to another world with thee? No, no, and why then dost thou set thine affections upon them when they are not thy goods to carry with thee wherever thou goest? If thou wouldst set thine affections upon grace and upon God, thou shouldst set thine affections upon thy goods; these are thy goods as long as thou livest, and these are thy goods when thou diest, and these thou mayst carry with thee whithersoever thou goest. "Wilt thou set thine eyes upon that which is not?" says Solomon; "for riches certainly make themselves wings, they fly away as an eagle,"

Proverbs 23:5. "Wilt thou set thine affections upon that which is not?" Wealth is not, and pleasure is not, and all the things of this world are not; they make themselves wings. Now maybe they are a bird in the hand, but by and by they are gone. There's a wing of prodigality, a wing of change, and of mishaps and of casualties, wings of losses and other occurrences, and though thou couldst clip all these wings with thy wisdom, yet the wing of death and mortality will carry them all away in a moment, and then whose shall they be? Thy pleasures, then whose shall they be? Thy gains and thy comings in, whose shall they be? Sure it is, they shall be none of thine, and therefore set thine affections elsewhere; thou must set them upon God.

Thirdly, they are not thy good, because they will not take thy part. Will any man set his affections on him that will not take his part? How can I affect him that will not affect me? If he will leave me in the lurch, I can never affect him as my friend. Alas! All the things of this life will leave thee in the lurch; thou mayst perish and be damned for all of them. They will never deliver thee from the hand of hell. When thou comest before the tribunal of Christ, dost thou think it will profit thee to say, "Lord, I have hunted and hawked, and gamed and sported, and I have been merry"? Will it benefit thee to say, "Lord, I have built and purchased, and increased my livings and my rents, I have a good house, and a good farm, and good friends"? Will this advantage thee? No, miserable comforters are they all. Canst thou say, "Lord, I have built up thy Church and thy worship, I have purchased zeal and holiness, and pureness, and glory to thy name, I have been persecuted and hated of all men for thy Name sake, and I am in Christ, etc."? If thou canst say thus, this would be thy good indeed. But if thou canst not say thus, though thou beest Gallinae filius albae, thou mayst perish with the devils and cursed fiends forevermore for all the blessings of this life. Set thine affections then upon God. Truly,

God is good to Israel, says the Psalmist, Psalms 73:1. He is good, and He truly is good. Thou canst not say so of all the things under Heaven. Thou canst not say, "Truly, riches are good to me. Pleasure truly is good to me. Peace and plenty and liberty truly are good to thee." They are good, but they will never be good to thee. When thou hast most need of good, then they will leave thee in the lurch. These do thee no good then. This is the third; as nothing but God is good, so nothing is thy good, but God.

Fourthly, as nothing is thy good but God, so nothing can rest thine affections but God. When thou affectest anything, wherefore dost thou affect it, but only to rest contented therewith when thou hast it? And therefore thou must set thine affections upon God, because nothing can rest thy soul but only thy God. "Rest in the Lord," Psalms 37:7. "Return unto thy rest, O my soul," Psalms 116:7. God is the rest of the soul; if the soul ever get Him, it resteth content. The affections are in a maze, if they be not set upon God, like a man in a quagmire, he sinks deeper and deeper. So a man sinks deeper and deeper in desires and in wishes, that hath not his affections upon God; there is nothing can give the soul rest, if the soul rest not in God. Will meat in a dream, and drink in a dream give satisfaction to our hunger and our thirst? So are all the good things in this world, Isaiah 29:8. Go to all the wicked men in the earth, let them desire and have their desires, still they desire and further their desire, and yet they desire after millions of desires; their affections are as far for to seek for rest, as if never they had sought. All the things in the world are like some ale-house-beer, which will never quench the poor traveller's thirst, like the eating of salt neats-tongues; the more they do eat, the more they are athirst: hungry meat, "He that desireth silver shall never be satisfied with silver; he that affects pleasure and vanity shall never be contented nor satisfied therewith." Give him ones, he affects tens; give him tens, he affecteth hundreds; give him hundreds, he affects thousands; give him them, he affecteth millions; thou canst never get rest till thine affections are pitched upon God. "Quo plus sunt potae, plus sitiuntur aquae." It's God only that resteth the affections. Now if these be so, is it not our best way to set our affections on God, where we may have rest for our souls? Nothing besides can give us any rest.

Firstly, because nothing but God is all good. Every good besides God hath but one or two goodnesses in it. None but God hath all goodnesses in him. What is meat good for, but only to feed one? When thou hast it, thou must desire again to have raiment, for meat will not clothe thee. What is raiment good for, but only to cover one? When thou hast it, thou must desire again to be fed, for raiment will not feed thee. What is money good for, but only to buy with? When thou hast it, thou must desire again to be recovered of thy sickness, for money will not cure thee of the fever. Thus, no good thing in the world can give thine affections a rest because they have but one or two goodnesses apiece in them. But the Lord's goodness is infinite; He is all good. If thou hast Him, thou wantest no manner of thing that is good. "They that seek the Lord shall not want any good thing," Psalms 34:10, for every good thing is in Him. He is bread to the hungry, and drink to the thirsty, and health to the sick, and liberty to the captive, all in all to them that set their affections on Him. "Frustra fit per plura quod fieri potest per pauciora." If thine affections go to any creature, thou fetchest but a little good at once; thine affections will be fain to go a thousand and a thousand times over and over. Thou gettest so little at once that thou shalt be tempted to be affecting the oftener. But if thine affections go to God, thou goest to the fountain. There thou hast it by drops, never enough; here thou mayst have it at once. Who would be so mad to fetch water at a cock that runneth by drops when the fountain is by?

Secondly, because nothing but God is the ultimate good. Thou affectest the things of this life, alas! They will never give rest, for still there is something beyond them, but God is the utmost of all goods. When the soul is once settled on Him, it hath no further to go, like a stone when it's come to the centre, it hath no further to go. "I am Alpha and Omega, the beginning and the end, the first and the last," says Christ. If the soul be in Christ, Christ is his last, the soul is at rest. Why? It hath nowhere to go. "Whither should we go?" says Peter to Christ, "thou hast the words of eternal life," John 6. Christ first, and Christ next, and Christ last; Christ is the utmost and ultimate good of the soul. The soul hath no further to go. Therefore, here thou must fix thine affections, fix them upon Christ.

Thirdly, because nothing is itself without God. The things of this life, they are good, I confess, but they are not themselves without God. If God be not in them, the very good that they have is not in them. When thou affectest pleasure and delight, answer me, why dost thou affect it? Is it not for the good that is in it? When thou affectest profit, or health, or peace, or friends, or credit, or whatever thou affectest, tell me in thy conscience, why dost thou affect them? Is it not for the good that is in them? They are good, therefore thou affectest them. But if thou hast not Christ, and God, and His Spirit, and His grace, if thou hast not the Lord in these things, they are not themselves, neither have they the good that is in them. Riches are no riches without grace, but a snare; health is no health without Christ, but a curse; peace and pleasure are not themselves without God, but poison; thy good parts are thy bane, thy money is thy vengeance, thy goods are a witness against thee without Christ. If thou beest not in Christ, if not a new creature, one day thou shalt curse that ever thou wert born, and therefore much more shalt thou curse that ever thou hadst means, or maintenance, or life, or health, or anything; the more thou hadst of these blessings, if Christ be not with them, as he is not, if thou beest not a new creature: I say, if Christ be not in them, the blessings are not themselves: they have not the good that is in them without Christ. David had a castle, and a buckler, and a horn, but they were not themselves without God. "Lord, thou art my castle, and my buckler, and the horn of my salvation." David had a servant to make his bed in his sickness, but to let us know that this blessing was not itself without God, he puts the phrase upon God, who made his bed in his sickness. No blessing is itself without Christ or without God. He hath all the goodness that is in it. The heathens have a pretty phrase, whereby they set out a happy man, "Vndecunque Deus," when God is everywhere about him; about him in his means and his riches, about him in his house and in his goods, about him in his friends and acquaintance, about him in his pleasure and mirth. He is not happy unless God be in everything that is about him. They are but the carcasses of good, if God be not in them. Thus you see we must set our affections on God.

Here then we are taught, That it is the blessing of God that we have affections implanted in our hearts. For how could they be set upon God, if it were not a blessing that we have them? There is a main controversy between the philosophers, the Stoics, and the Peripatetics, concerning the affections. The Stoics do stiffly maintain that it is an evil to have any affections at all. Therefore, Zeno defines the affections to be unnatural stirrings of the heart, averse from right reason, which is false. For this is the definition of affections, as they are corrupt, and not as they are affections. The affections in themselves are not sinful.

First, because Adam and Eve had affections in innocence. If the affections were all sinful in themselves, Adam and Eve in their innocence could not have had them, for they were created without sin. But they were created with affections, such as love, joy, delight, hope, fear, and the like. Before Eve ever sinned, we see plainly she was afraid to eat of the forbidden fruit. Indeed, when the devil had ripened his temptation, then she went fearlessly on to eat it. But when the devil assaulted her at first, she said, "We may not eat of it, lest we die," Genesis 3:3. Lo, she was afraid to eat it at first. I confess that before the fall, they may not have had all the affections in act because there were no objects for all the affections to work on. They had nothing to grieve for, nothing to be angry at, nothing to despair of. But for my part, I think they had distinct objects to work on, though not in themselves. For they had not sinned as yet, yet they had distinct objects in the world for all their affections to work on. Should they not grieve to see God dishonoured by the fall of the angels? Should they not hate and abhor backsliding from God? Though there were none in themselves, nevertheless, the affections of fear and hatred were given to them to keep away sin and apostasy from God. Now if the affections were in Adam in innocence, they could not be sinful in themselves.

Secondly, because Christ took our affections upon him. If the affections were sinful in themselves, he could not take our affections upon him, for he was made like unto us, sin only excepted. Therefore, if the affections were sins, he could not have taken our affections. But he did take them, as the Gospel abundantly shows. He had our affection of joy, for "Jesus rejoiced in spirit, and said, I thank thee, O Father," Luke 10:23. He had our affection of sorrow, for "My soul is exceeding sorrowful unto death," Matthew 26:38. He had our affection of anger: "He looked round about on them with anger, being grieved at their hardness of heart," Mark 3:5. He had our affection of desire, for "With desire I have desired to eat this Passover with you before I suffer," Luke 22:15. And so on. If Christ took our affections upon him, our affections are not sinful in themselves. Moreover, he did not only, as the Son of man, take our primitive affections as we are men, but he was "Ben Enosh," he was the son of frail man, Psalm 8:5. And he took our miserable affections, our affections of infirmity, upon him. I do not mean the affections of sinful infirmity, for he knew no sin. But I mean the affections of our frailty and infirmity, such as fear, fellow-feeling, and the like. "For we have not a high priest who cannot be touched with the feeling of our infirmities, but was in all points tempted like as we are, yet without sin," Hebrews 4:15. This then is an undeniable argument that the affections are not sinful in themselves, because Christ did assume them.

Thirdly, because the Lord commands us to be angry. "Be angry and sin not," says he. He commands us to grieve and be sorry for our sins. "Therefore also now saith the Lord, Turn ye even to me with all your heart, and with fasting, and with weeping, and with mourning," Joel 2:12. He commands us to fear. "Work out your salvation with fear and trembling; pass the time of your sojourning here in fear. Be not high-minded, but fear." "I will forewarn you," says Christ, "whom ye shall fear; fear him which after he hath killed, hath power to cast into hell; yea, I say unto you, fear him," Luke 13:5. He commands us to be ashamed of our evil doings, and is offended if we are not. "Thou hast a whore's forehead, and refusest to be ashamed," Jeremiah 3:3. If the affections were sinful in themselves, the Lord would not command us to show our affections in this way. It's true, they are sinfully used and corruptly perverted among men. The more is the pity, but they are not so in themselves. Neither do I deny that there are some natural affections that are naturally sinful in themselves, such as envy and malice, which never can be regulated or guided by any moderation but are to be utterly rooted out. But these affections are not properly natural; they are no otherwise natural than lice and vermin are natural to carrion, than filthy and noisome weeds are natural to a cursed ground. These must be utterly rooted up and stubbed out of our hearts because, to speak properly, they are unnatural affections and sinful in themselves. But our natural affections are not sinful in themselves. Nay more, let me tell you, the affections are not only not sinful, but it is an infinite blessing of God that God has given us affections.

Firstly, if we had no affections at all, we should be like stocks and senseless stones. The philosopher was in doubt whether Brutus were not a block or a brute because he had no affection at all for his own children, whom he could see murdered before him with dry eyes. The Lord Himself counts that man a very block who has no affection in his heart. "Have ye no regard, all ye that pass by? Behold and see if there were any sorrow like my sorrow," Lamentations 1:12. (That is to say,) Are you such blocks and stupid stocks that you can show no affection at my sorrow? Therefore, it's reckoned among the symptoms of a heart that is desperately hardened not to be affected by anything: to hear the Word and not be affected by it, to pray to God and not be affected by His presence, to be in affliction and not be affected by remorse. This is a symptom of a hard heart. Therefore, it is a blessing of God that a man has affections within him.

Secondly, because, as Plutarch, the very Heathen observes, were it not for our affections, our nature would be lazy and idle, like a pilot at sea without wind. Alas! The ship would go slowly were there no winds stirring to drive it. So the affections, says he, are to the soul as the wind to the sails of the ship. As the ship could not sail apace without winds, so the soul would go slowly about anything if the affections did not carry it. When David's affections were hampered about with worldly fears, fears of his enemies and griefs at his persecutions which he suffered, he went slowly on in obedience. But as soon as his sails were up, then he ran like a ship in the sea with a great wind, "I will run the way of thy commandments, when thou shalt enlarge my heart," Psalm 119:32. As soon as God would help him to spread the sails of his heart and enlarge his affections, then he would run like a fleet pinnace in the seas. "I will then run the way of thy commandments," says he. This is an infinite mercy of God who, seeing how dull we are unto good, how slack to good duties, how slow to holy performances, vouchsafes us these winds and these sails to carry us, says the same philosopher. The affections are like wheels and like chariots unto reason. If a man's reason be never so good, he knows he is bound to repent, be godly, and obey. Yet if he has no affections thereto, he goes like a chariot without wheels; he goes without force, he cannot go at all. But if he has affections thereto, the affections are like wheels and like horses to carry him amain. "Draw me," says the Christian soul unto Christ, "draw me, and I will run after thee," Song of Solomon 1:4. She prays that Christ would draw her by the affections of love, for she speaks of love; "the virgins love thee," says she. "Draw me with thy love too, and then I shall run after thee," like the chariots of Aminadab, that is, drawn by quick horses. She would run as with wheels unto Christ if her affections did once carry her. As Cicero says of the affections of anger, it is the whetstone to valour. So I may say of all the affections, they are all whetstones to good, if a man has any grace. Hast thou love? It is a whetstone to obedience. Hast thou grief? It is a whetstone to repentance. Hast thou anger? It is a whetstone to zeal, etc. Why do men come so slowly to good? The reason is this: because their affections stand another way. Men repent slowly, amend their lives slowly, increase in grace slowly. Why? This is the cause: their affections are to the world; they run on in their pleasures, their vanities, their earthly employments, and businesses. Why? Their affections are thereto. O beloved, it is an infinite mercy of God that we have affections given us by God, for these may quicken our dullness unto grace.

Thirdly, because the affections are good channels for grace to run down in. Be there never so full a fountain of good water, yet if it have not a channel to run all along in, the fountain may be ever bubbling, but it chokes itself for want of a channel. So though God should put never so much grace into thy heart, yet if it should have no channel to run down in, it would smother itself. Now God has given thee affections like channels for grace to run down in. Art thou covetous and full of desires? What a fine channel is that for grace to run down in? It is the easier for thee to covet the best things. Art thou of a choleric and angry constitution? What a fine channel is that for zeal for God's glory to run down in? It is the easier for thee to be zealous in God's worship. Art thou melancholy and of a sad disposition? What a fine channel is that for repentance to run down in? It is the easier for thee to despise the vain pleasures of the world and to sorrow for sin. Art thou merry and of a cheerful nature? What a fine channel is this for delight in the Lord to run down in? It is the easier for thee to joy in the Holy Ghost. Art thou fearful and of a timorous spirit? What a fine channel is that for fear of God's judgments and truth to run down in? It is the easier for thee to tremble before God and fear to offend him.

Solomon was full of the affections of love, it is true; he let lust after women and uncleanness a while run down in that channel. But when grace and repentance recovered his soul, what an excellent channel was it for love unto Christ to run down in? Never was there such a lovesong to Christ as the Canticles since the creation of the world to this day. And therefore it is called the Song of Songs. Certainly, Jeremiah was a man of a sad constitution, but see what an advantage this bent of affection was to him. It was a channel for spiritual sadness to run down in. "Oh, that my head were waters, and mine eyes a fountain of tears, to weep day and night for the slain of the daughter of my people," Jeremiah 9:1. The woman in the Gospel who was a sinner, a whore in plain terms, one bewitched with the affections of love to her lovers; as soon as ever any grace did look into her heart, see how these affections of love did advantage her. She loved our Saviour more affectionately than Saint Peter himself. "She loved much," says the text, Luke 7:47. Before, no question but she was full of her whorish and strumpet-like tears; now the channel was turned, she washed Christ's feet with her tears and wiped them with the hair of her head; "and she loved much," says the text. It is such an admirable advantage to be full of affections that the Lacedaemonian schoolmaster thought that if he had a young scholar full of affections, full of shamefastness, and full of fear, and full of cheerfulness, etc., he thought it was easy for him to make him ashamed of all filthiness, and delighted in goodness, and fearful to do evil. I am not of his mind, but this I am though, he has an exceeding good advantage to do it. If a man has spent his affections upon sin and eaten out the heart of his affections upon vanity, or if a man has no affections at all, as some have but few, a man shall as soon work on a beast as such a man. Nay, if grace should come into such a man, alas! He shall never be able to come to much good. If the best come to the best, he shall have infinite ado to do any duty without woeful dullness and senselessness. It is an admirable blessing that God gives unto men to give them affections, and therefore the Stoics are infinitely to blame to cry out against the affections as if they were evil in themselves. To speak truly and rightly of the Stoics, I do not think the Stoics were ever so sottish as to mean so; but their intent, as Augustine says of them, was to pare off the affections that are evil and to rule the affections that are natural. And therefore it was that they declaimed so bitterly against the affections. You see now by this text I have chosen that the affections are great gifts of the Lord, for how could the Apostle command us to set our affections upon God if the affections were evil in themselves? Nay, it follows from hence that it is a great blessing of God that we have any affections at all, that we may set them upon God.

THE FIFTH SERMON.

"Set your affections on things that are above, and not on things which are on the earth." – Colossians 3:2

The Christians of the Primitive Church had learnt this lesson very well, to set their affections on God's Kingdom. They were often thinking of it, often speaking of it in the companies they came in. They would be discoursing of it, insomuch that the foolish Heathen, hearing them talking so often of a Kingdom, took them for affecters of Kingdoms and accused them of aspiring to be Kings. "Ye hear," says Justin Martyr, "that we expect for a Kingdom. Ye imagine we look after human Kingdoms. No, No," says he, "we mean the Kingdom with God and with Christ in Heaven above." Their affections were much there.

You have heard, beloved, the necessity of this duty, that we must set our affections upon God and his Kingdom and grace. You have heard the reasons why we must do so. For the use of the point, you have heard a confutation of the Stoics, that teach a vacuity of affections, and say the affections are all evil in themselves. They cannot be evil in themselves because we must set them upon God. Were they evil in themselves, it would be unlawful to set them upon God. But it is not only not unlawful, but also it is very necessary to set our affections upon God.

Oh, this is a hard duty to our corrupt flesh, and so you shall find it, to set your affections on God. There are many obstacles that hinder us from doing so.

Firstly, it is a very hard thing to turn an antipathy or a sympathy; our hearts are so deeply affected with the things of the world that they have a sympathy with them and an antipathy against a removal therefrom. When the affections are deeply set with or against, they prove to be sympathies and antipathies, which are infinitely hard to be changed. The Philosophers call them "occultae qualitates," hidden qualities; no reason can be given for them. No man can give a reason why the load-stone should be so deeply affected with iron as to draw it unto it. It hath a sympathy with it; the wild Bull hath a sympathy with a fig tree; nothing can tame him but it; the Elm hath a sympathy with the Vine: the Vine hath a sympathy with the Olive. No man can give a reason why it should be so. So beloved, our deep affections are the sympathies of our hearts, and therefore, seeing they are set to the things of the world, they are hardly removed. No reason, scarcely any reason can sever them. Demas, when he set his love upon the world, the text says he forsook Paul, and he embraced this present world, "Demas hath forsaken me, and embraced this present world" (2 Tim. 4:10). We translate it, he loved this present world, but the word signifies, and so other translations render it, he embraced this present world; that is, the affections of his heart had a sympathy with it, as the Ivy with the Elm, he embraced it. Saint Paul could not hold him, no reason could withhold him, he had a sympathy with it. Now when the heart hath a sympathy with the things of the world, it must needs have an antipathy at grace; the proud man hath an antipathy at the parting with that which he prides in; the revengeful man hath an antipathy at the putting up of an injury. The stubborn man hath an antipathy at a sound reproof; he cannot endure to be sharply rebuked for his sins. As some men (suffer a homely similitude), I say, have an antipathy with Cheese, they will go out of the room where it is. As the mullet hath an antipathy with the Pike; the Coleworts have an antipathy with the Vine; they will die rather than grow together. So men are vexed to be curbed of their lusts. The affections are the sympathies and the antipathies of the heart, and therefore, it's very hard to remove them; it will cost thee a mighty deal of labor to pull off thine affections from all the things in the world and to set them upon God.

Secondly, it is a hard thing to work on the heart when the heart is bewitched. The affections are the bewitchings of the heart; when the heart hath once set its affections on the things of the World, it is even quite bewitched therewith. Foolish people talk much of bewitchings; Brethren let me tell you, here's a bewitching ye little consider. Your affections bewitch you. "O foolish Galatians, who hath bewitched you, that ye should not obey the truth?" (Gal. 3:1). "Anathema," says Saint Chrysostom. This is the bewitching of the devil; the false Apostles had wrought upon the Galatians affections and drawn them from the truth, and now when their affections were set on it, the Apostle says they were bewitched. The affections when once they are up about a thing that is earthly or carnal, they are like a company of devils in hell to bewitch one; there be abundance of bewitchings in nature. The bird Galgalus, if she sees a man that is sick of the Jaundies, the man recovers, and she is so bewitched therewith that she dieth. If a Toad be seen by the Wesil to gape, the Wesil is so bewitched, that she gives up herself to be devoured; but of all the bewitchings in the world, the bewitching of the affections is the most dangerous. Eucilides was in so deep an affection to his own beauty that he was bewitched with it: were not Samson's affections bewitched with Delilah? Were not Herod's affections bewitched with Herodias? Were not Judas' affections bewitched with the gain of thirty pence, that for it he should deny his own Master? Saint Paul tells the Galatians their affections were bewitched. Saint Jerome thinks verily the devil was in them. The Drunkard is bewitched with his cups; the Adulterer with his whore, the angry man with his choler, the vain man with his vanities, the carnal man with his flesh; that they will damn their own souls, rather than be new creatures. Beloved, are not ye bewitched in your sins when all the preaching and teaching and warning ye have had, cannot yet turn you from your sins unto God, to set your affections above? This is a grievous let that sends millions to hell, their affections bewitch them. Ye need no Devils to tempt you to sin: if your affections be once set on it, they will bewitch you as bad as any devil can bewitch you. Nay, the devil cannot bewitch you to sin, but only by your affections. If ever thou save thy soul, thou shalt find it a great task to unbewitch thine affections, to set them upon grace.

Thirdly, another hindrance is that as the affections are the bewitchings of the heart, so they are the estimations of the heart. If the thing is not good enough to be affected, which the affections are set on, they esteem it worthy to be affected. "Quisquis amat ranam, ranam putat esse Dianam." Many of you know the old proverb: If a man should set his affections on a frog, there's little goodness in a Frog, why it should be affected; but if a man should set his affections on a Frog, he would esteem it as comely, as another would Diana. The affections, if they are set upon vanity, they do utterly besot one. Look upon the Drunkard, he thinks it's a fine life to be potting and piping in the Ale-house: which a man in his wits knows to be base and brutish, and hellish. Look upon the vain Gentleman, he thinks it a fine life to be hunting and gambolling and bragging and flaunting, and challenging, and to be served and to be worshipped at every word. Which a wise man knows to be foppish, and foolish, and devilish. The affections blind the judgment, and befool the understanding, and make a man defend himself in a course which in very deed will lead him to hell. When the children of Israel had set their affections on their lusts; Moses thus speaks to them. "Do ye thus requite the Lord, ye foolish people and unwise? Is not he thy Father?" (Deut. 32:6). Natural affection would lead a child to be obedient to his father, and seeing their affections were cross set, the Lord calls them a foolish people. Their sinful affections did besot them and befool them. Samosatenus was so besotted with the love of a certain woman, that he forsook his faith and religion for her. I read of a pretty parable to this purpose. When Ulysses had left his men with Circe the witch, she changed them all into diverse sorts of beasts, Dogs, Swine, Lions, Tigers, Ulysses complained she had done him great wrong for changing his men into beasts on that fashion: "wrong?" says she: "I have not done thee nor them any wrong. Do but ask them now whether they do not like the condition they are in." So Ulysses demanded first of the Hog, whether he would be a man again or not. He answered no, by no means; For now he could fill his belly, and lie down on the dunghill and sleep. And so he demanded of the rest, and they all save only the Elephant, they all replied they had rather be beasts as now they were. This parable is made to show how the carnal affections besot one, to esteem the pleasures of sin, the gains and profits and beggarly things of the World, and prefer them before holiness, and righteousness, and pureness, and strictness of living. One, his affections besot him in a love-lock or long hair, that he cannot be persuaded to shave it off: another, his affections besot him in a Tobacco-pipe, another in a filthy gotten custom, another in some other base haunt of the heart, all the preaching under Heaven cannot dissuade them, therefore they do so esteem them and prize them, and think they are so pleasing: a noble-minded Christian would wonder how it is possible they can so.

Fourthly, another hindrance is that as the affections are the estimations of the heart, so they are the most natural temperaments of the heart. Spiritual and heavenly affections are the good temper of the heart, and carnal or earthly affections are the evil temper of the heart, and therefore it's hard to change one's affections, because the heart itself must be taken to pieces as it were, if one would alter his affections. An earthly heart is not a right soil for the spiritual plants to grow in. Gardeners have daily experience what a coil they have to keep an herb from dying in their gardens, when the garden is not a right soil for it: they are fain for to dig it, and dress it, and water it, and tend it, yet scarce will it grow there when it is not a right soil for it. Men must get themselves new hearts and new minds, if ever they would have their affections renewed. "Fashion not yourselves to the world," says the Apostle, "but be ye transformed by the renewing of your mind" (Rom. 12:2). Unless your mind be renewed, ye can never spy a pleasing fashion of the world, but O your affections will be to it. When David had misplaced his affections on Bathsheba another man's wife, and his affections had been mad upon adultery, and on murder, what does he do? He goes to God in prayer for a new heart, he could never have new affections else; "Create in me a clean heart, O God, and renew a right spirit within me" (Psa. 51:10). He could not get new affections, till he had gotten a new heart. This is a miserable impediment that lets multitudes of men and women from setting their affections upon God; because their hearts are not a right for such affections as these. Maybe they trim their affections, as the very heathens have done, with morality; as a Barber trims and shaves a man's head, but the hair grows again, because the head is the hair's soil. So the carnal affections will grow again: spiritual and heavenly affections will not grow there, for the heart is not a right soil: and this is a shrewd let, and you must labor continually to remove it.

And therefore, before I help you with means how to set your affections on God, let me give you these two grounds.

First, You must have this same new heart, otherwise you cannot set your affections on God. For there is a heart that will set its affections on God, and there is a heart that will not. The Lord wishes his people to have the former kind of heart, the heart that will set its affections on God. "O that there were such a heart in them, that they would fear me, and keep my Commandments always" (Deut. 5:29). There is such a heart, beloved. O that we had it; I say, there is such a heart that will fear God and set all its affections on God; and such a heart you must get, or else it is in vain to command you this duty: all the Sermons (you see) are in vain that you have heard to this day; all the exhortations and admonitions you have had since you were, you see plainly they are in vain to many of you: as your affections were earthly twenty years ago, so they are still; as they were carnal and worldly heretofore, so they are still; your hearts are the same hearts, your hearts are stark naught, and therefore your affections cannot soar up unto God. You can have no quick affections in prayer, no melting affections at the word: The Sabbath comes, but your affections are not on it: a Sacrament comes, but what poor affections you have to it, your consciences may witness. You sit in your shops, or you follow your callings, or you go about your earthly employments, and your affections are below; "ἀσπίς," says Maximus, the Sparrows foot is bound with a cord, she cannot fly up unto God. Your hearts are not spiritual, and this is the cause your affections are so carnal. Perhaps you lop off now and then some part of your carnal affections, as Tarquinius lopped off the heads of his poppies, but you do not cut up the roots. It may be you go about to heave up your affections in good duties sometimes, as the key lifts up the spring in the lock, but the key is no sooner turned but down goes the spring, so down go your affections presently again. And therefore I premise this as a first ground, you can never set your affections on God until you have gotten new hearts.

The second ground is this, you can never set your affections upon God unless you feed upon Christ by faith. If ever the soul feeds upon Christ by faith, it cannot but set its affections upon God. I remember an invention of Queen Artemesia, who when her husband Mausolus was dead, not knowing how to keep him fresh in her affections as long as she lived, she caused her husband Mausolus his body to be turned into ashes, and mingled them in her drink; so she buried her husband in her bowels, and this way she took to keep her affections fresh unto him. This indeed was unnatural in her, to eat and drink her own husband; but faith teaches us to feed upon the Lord Jesus Christ: this will take off our affections from the world, we shall never hunger after the world more, nor thirst after the things of this life more, if ever we feed upon him. "I am the bread of life," says Christ, "he that cometh to me shall never hunger, and he that believeth on me shall never thirst" (John 6:35). If ever we believe the sweetness of the promises of Christ, the pleasantness of the commandments of Christ, the preciousness of the graces of Christ, and the love of Christ, and the benefit of Christ, our affections will be to him. Nothing can take off your affections from the world but faith in Christ. He that believeth in Christ cannot set his affections upon the world. Can a man set his affections upon the world when he verily believes it to be dross and dung in comparison of Christ? Can he set his affections upon earthly pleasure, that believes it is madness? It is certain, men never believed in Christ since they were born, that set their affections upon the things of the world; they have not one dram of Christ. Christ is altogether lovely. "He is all love, one that commands the affections." You believe in the world and not in Christ if you set your affections upon any other but Christ. You believe you can have pleasure and delight in something beside Christ, profits and gains in something beside Christ; ease, and content, and comfort in something beside Christ; if you set your affections upon anything beside Christ. Alas! You can never set your affections upon Christ as long as you believe not only in Christ. If your earthly affections transport you to be earthly, fly under the wing of Christ, as Chickens under the wing of the Hen, lest the Kite devour them. These are the two Grounds that I give you. First, you must have new hearts: and secondly, you must be believers in Christ, or else you cannot set your affections upon God.

The foundation being laid, let me now help you with some means to set your affections on God. I could provide you with an abundance of means, but I desire to offer you those that are easier to use than to set your affections on God. For if they are not easier than this duty, they cannot properly be said to be helps to this duty.

The first, then, is this: Often pray to God that he would gather up our affections from the things of the world and unite them unto him. Our hearts are divided and scattered up and down among the things of the world. Carnal friends have some of your affections; our gains, our livings, and our maintenance have others; our pleasures, delights, and fleshly refreshments have more; our earthly businesses, cares, employments, our credit, and the like: these have abundance of our affections. Thus, our hearts and affections are scattered up and down among the things of the world; if ever we would have them set upon God, we must be frequent in prayer; that God would unite together our scattered hearts to set our affections upon God. This was the practice of David, "O Lord," says he, "unite my heart to fear thy name" (Psa. 86:11). His heart was scattered up and down in a thousand pieces. Some pieces of his affections run after one thing, some after another. And therefore he prays God to unite his heart together, to fear his Name. If God would once gather up his heart from all its vain haunts and unite it together; then he could set his affections, his fear, his love, his delight, and the rest, upon God's Name. "Iejunio passions corporis, oratione pestes sanandae sunt mentis," says Jerome; as the affections of the body are to be healed by fasting, so the affections of the soul are to be healed by prayer: as long as they are carnal, they are the plague and pestilence of the soul, and prayer must heal them. As Father Latimer said to good Ridley, "pray, pray, O pray, pray"; so may I say, "Pray, pray, I beseech you, pray unto God evermore, again, I say, pray." "I have not time to pray so often," you object. "I do pray in the morning and evening, but my businesses are so many," etc. Not enough time, you say? Find out some odd times besides morning and evening: steal into some corner or other, belabour your heart before God. "O," you say, "I find it a hard thing to stir up my affections, I am a very Stoic, ἀπαθής, I have no affection, I cannot compel my affections to God." Can you not? But you can compel your heart to pray; you can tug and pull at your heart in your prayers, and this will fetch up your affections. Prayer is not only a mouth to beg Physic, but also it is Physic itself, whereby Christ cures the affections of the heart. The poor beggar, the more he is driven to beg, the more affectionate he is in describing his miseries: you shall see some beggars to set forth their misery, and cry so lamentably, as it would burst a man's heart with pity and compassion, one's bowels would even yearn but to hear them. I do not mean your lazy canting beggars, but distressed Lazars indeed. So beloved, pray; if ever you are used to it, it will screw up your heart and raise up your affections exceedingly. I do not mean that lazy-hearted and canting kind of praying of most wretches, that has no more affection in it than there is savor in the white of an Egg. But set yourself to prayer indeed, and by it Christ will quicken your affections. Alas! Your heart is divided and scattered up and down among the things of the world, and therefore strive with God that he would gather up all the pieces into one; you must have all your affections and all the pieces of your heart gathered up into one if you would set them upon God. "I will give them one heart that they may fear me forever," says God, Jer. 32:39 your heart and the affections of your heart are divided and scattered up and down into a thousand pieces, one upon one thing, another upon another; and God has promised that he will gather up your hearts into one and give you this same one heart, that you may fear him and set all your affections upon him; will you miss such a gracious promise as this for want of asking it, and begging it, and praying for it? This is the reason why men have such earthly affections as they have because they are not frequent in prayer to God to be helped! Prayer is an excellent help to wind up your affections to God. This is the first, Often prayer to God.

The second is this, Light up a candle in your heart, that it may see what to set your affections on in God. Get knowledge of God: "Ignoti nulla cupido," unknown unaffected; your affections are unruly, and you cannot rule them towards God, yet you can get knowledge. Knowledge will help you exceedingly. We plainly see that affections closest to reason are easiest to control. And those farthest from reason are more challenging to rule. A man commonly will sooner control his affections rightly than a woman or a child because a man has more reason. Philosophers illustrate this with the example of a Horse or a Bul. A Horse is sooner tamed than a Fish because a Horse is more capable of knowledge and reason; as natural reason and knowledge can naturally rule the affections, so spiritual reason and knowledge can spiritually rule the affections. And therefore, if you would rule your affections rightly to set them on God, labour to know God. "Everyone that loveth God knoweth God" (1 John

4:7). He must indeed know God who loves God, for how can he set his affections of love upon God if he does not know God? "Knowing therefore the terror of the Lord, we persuade men" (2 Corinthians 5:11). St. Paul persuades the affections of the people, why? Because he knew the terror of the Lord, and he was able to make them know it too; and therefore hereby he endeavoured to persuade their affections to fear God and to serve him. "They that know thy Name will put their trust in thee, for thou never forsakest them that seek thee" (Psalms 9:10). David speaks peremptorily, they that know thy Name, they will place their hope, trust, confidence, and all their affections on thee. They will do so certainly if they know thee, if once they know what a good God thou art, how true to thy promise, how gracious to thy children, how sure a friend thou art, never forsaking them that seek thee. He concludes it positively, they that know God will set their affections on God. Can a covetous man know a rich purchase and not have an affection for it? Can a beggar know his alms are a hundred pounds and have no affection to take it? As long as the woman of Samaria did not know Christ, she stood prattling and wrangling and jeering at Christ, she had no affection neither to him nor the water of life that he could give her, she had more mind of her well, and her water-pot: though she were in Christ's company, yet because she did not know, she never asked him a drop of grace, nor would she give so much as a draught of her water to Christ. But what answer did he make to her? "If thou knewest," says he, "who it is that saith to thee, give me to drink, thou wouldest have asked of him, and he would have given thee living water" (John 4:10). If you had known who I am, your affections would have been eagerer than they are. Beloved, you hear the word, and have no affection to tremble at it. You hear God's Commandments, and have no affection to do them, you live in your sins, many of you poor damned souls to this day, and you have no affection to be humbled. Alas! Alas! You are blind, and you know not. But if you had known what a damnable case you are in, what a word it is you reject, whose Commandments they are which you break, whose blood it is you contemn; if you had known God and the truth that is of God, you would have been otherwise affected than you are. "Occultae musices nullus respectus," says Suetonius. Be the music never so pleasing, yet if it is not known, none is affected therewith. You will say you do know God; what do? And have no more affections to obey the Commandments of God? You lie in fiat terms, says St. John. "He that saith I know him, and keeps not his Commandments, is a liar, and there is no truth in him" (1 John 2:4). I confess you may know many things about God and never have your affections set upon God to obey him; but this knowledge is in a reprobate, there's no truth in this knowledge. "The truth is not in him," says the Text. Knowledge may be in him, but the truth of knowledge is not in him. And if you do not know God, no marvel though your affections are not set on him. "Incognitum non amatur," Unknown unkissed, as we say. This is the second help to set our affections on God, to know God.

The third is this, Occasion your affections this way, Be it never so hard to overcome corrupt nature to set your affections upon God, it is easier a great deal to give them frequent occasions to be set upon God. A thievish companion, maybe, is afraid to steal, lest he should be taken, yet if a booty do ever and anon offer itself pretty handsomely and fairly and covertly unto him, then he will steal it.

Occasion facit furem, Occasion makes a filcher; the postern door maketh a thief, as the Proverb is. That gives him an occasion for his villainy; as it is in evil, so also in good. Occasion your affections always to good, at last they may take hold of it. Be often thinking, and meditating, and remembering of God, let your thoughts and meditations give occasion to your heart, in the end it may take it. The Apostle gives this as a reason why Titus was so well affected with the good people in Corinth, namely, because he thought of and remembered their obedience to God. His inward affection is the more abundant toward you, whilst he remembereth the obedience of you all, 2 Cor. 7:15. if we would often busy our thoughts and remembrances of God, this might win our affections to God. You give your affections so many thousand occasions to be set upon the things of this life, your tongue is accustomed to speak of little else, your ear accustomed to hear little else, your mind and your memory accustomed to think of little else, you give your heart so many occasions to set its affections on the things of this life, that I wonder not your affections are not set upon God. This is the reason why men are so touchy and so choleric, and revengeful and envious and malicious; this is the reason why they are so apt to be overtaken with inordinate pleasure, or covetous desires, or carnal sorrows and griefs and the like, they give their hearts occasions to be so; they are not choice of their company, they are not wary of the beginnings of sin, they entertain too many thoughts of injuries and crosses, and afflictions, and profits, and vanity in the world, many occasions they give to their hearts to set their affections thereon. The heart when it has an occasion to sin, is like the wild ass in the Prophet: in her occasion who can turn her away? Jer. 2:24. The wild ass if she have an occasion of lust, nobody can turn her away from her lust, as Tremellius observes: occasion is a main thing in matters either of sin or of grace. If Peter had not given his heart an occasion to be tempted by being in the Hall, doubtless he would have been better occupied then in denying his Master; if David had not given occasion to his lusts by looking carelessly from his roof, for all that I know, he had been at his prayers, when he was a whoring with Uriah his wife. If Lot had not given occasion to his flesh by drinking of Wine, he had been a blessing of God for his mercy the while he was committing of incest. Capillataest occasio, Occasion hath a foretop, how easy is it to be taken hold of? The Galatians are commanded, that their liberty be not used as an occasion to the flesh, Gal. 5:13. for as soon as the flesh has an occasion offered, presently it's likely to take it. Women must not give an occasion to the Adversary to speak reproachfully, 1 Tim. 5:14. Let no man put a stumbling block or an occasion to fall in his brothers way. Rom. 14:13. Occasions to evil are all dangerous, as the flesh is ready to take all occasion to sin, so the spirit to take an occasion to good. And therefore if you would set your affections on God, give your heart as many occasions that way as you can; keep such company as may occasion your heart to be affected with Christ. Compose yourself to be often thinking and meditating of the Word, and of such things as may occasion your heart to set its affections above. And when your heart has such occasions as these offered unto it, press it and urge it to take hold of the occasion. Premenda occasio, says Horace; good occasions are to be pressed upon. If you would make conscience of this duty, to occasion your affections aright, they would be set quickly upon God. This is the third help, to set your affections on God, give your affections often occasion that way.

The fourth is this. Let your affections be often wooed to God, never miss, if you can choose, the preaching of God's word: there is never a godly Minister but is Christ's paranymph, he is a friend of the Bridegroom, John 3:29. Whenever he preaches, he comes on Christ's errand to woo your affections to Christ. Christ acts as a great Prince, who, intending to marry a wife from a far Country, sends over his paranymphs to woo for him, to win her affections, if possible. So beloved, we who are God's Ministers, we are Christ's paranymphs, we preach to woo your affections to Christ. And therefore never miss the preaching of the Word, it's the wooing of your affections to Christ; they say, women love to be much wooed. Love then the preaching of the Word, that woos you and woos you again and again. Oh, what infinite need have you of coming continually to the Word; your affections are infinitely coy; this they must have, and that they must have. Like a vain Damsel, she must have her trinkets, and her fashions, she must have her pleasure and her will, and her ease, and thus it must be, and so it shall be, if she marry him, she will not have the man else. He has such difficulty in winning her affections, either he is too homely, or too base, or too strict, or too ill-favoured, or too poor, or something. Maybe he has her, and then her thoughts change, then again she is inclined, and then her affections are off. My brethren, so it is with our souls; our affections are for this and that and I know not what. If Christ will not let them have their pleasures, and their ease, and their profits, and their vanities, Christ is not for them. They must have the credit in the world, they'll not be mocked at for puritans and for hypocrites, they'll not deny father nor mother, nor self, nor any of these things, they are loath to be held in so strictly, as Christ does demand. But Christ will not marry us, unless our affections be wholly upon him. Blessed is he that is not offended in me. Many are offended at the preciseness of his word, many at the bitterness of the Cross, many at the shame of the world, they are offended in Christ, their affections are quite against these things. They are unwilling to always talk about Sermons and about Heaven, to always rack their thoughts about their sins, and about repentance and faith, to be hated by all men, to go through tribulations and persecutions for the Gospel's sake, to part with their customs, and their own natural inclinations and their lusts, their affections are against these conditions. Oh, it's wondrous hard to woo the affections of the heart unto Christ. And do you think that Christ will marry you till your affections come down to his conditions? Will a man marry a woman whom he sees is contrary-hearted unto him?

A cross wife is a tempest and a storm in a house. Come then continually to the preaching of the word, if ever you desire to have your affections wrought on. God's Ministers are Christ's paranymphs, they preach for this purpose to woo your affections to Christ. If there be any one Sermon that you refuse to attend when you may, your conscience tells you you may be at it, and will not, if there be any one Sermon, I say, that you will not be at, you reject Christ's paranymphs. Like a cross maid, that when her suitor comes to her, he shall have no speech with her, She will not be spoken with. Oh, what a provoking is this unto Christ? If you will not be spoken with, take heed lest the Lord Jesus abhor to own you. Nay, if she be so strange forsooth, let her keep her affections for who's will, I scorn to woo her any more. How long has Christ wooed your affections! Beloved, and yet he's pleased to woo you. Bring hither your affections, that here they may be wrought. Frequent the Lord's house, for here are Christ's paranymphs: if ever your affections can be won, here they may be won some time or other. Many other means may be used to help you in this task, namely, to set your affections on God. But these may suffice for the present. Set your affections on things that are above, and not on things that are on the earth.

The Sixth Sermon

"Set your affections on things that are above, and not on things which are on the earth." – Colossians 3:2

The fifth means to set our affections on God is to be sober and temperate in all things. For if we are not, our affections cannot steadfastly settle upon God. And this is the reason why the Apostle joins sobriety with prayer. Prayer is a duty that requires the utmost freedom of affections for God, and if it is not backed with sobriety, it will soon be without affection and lifeless, "Be ye sober and watch unto prayer," 1 Peter 4:7. Titus must exhort young men to be sober-minded, Titus 2:6. Young men's affections, you know, are more unruly than others, and therefore they need sobriety, otherwise their affections will be greatly excessive. If you take any recreation, take it very moderately: one little game of bowls, one hour's play at shovel-board, or at chess, or the like: if you do not take heed, it is strange how it will dull your affections to good duties; if you follow your business in the world, follow it soberly, do not be overly eager upon it, lest it dull your affections towards God. If you eat, drink, sleep, or talk, whatever you do, be sure to do it soberly. Beware of the slightest excess, lest your affections are suddenly enticed by it.

If you let your affections wander too much in this manner, they will quickly become mad. Either to make you intoxicated with the cares of this life, Luke 21:34. Or to be utterly intoxicated with pride, Isaiah 28:1. Intoxicated with pleasure, intoxicated with fury, and so forth. All drunkenness is not drunkenness with drink, says S. Jerome. A man's soul may be intoxicated with a passion, intoxicated with love, and intoxicated with hatred, and intoxicated with any other affection. Thus civil men, and sober men, as we call them, though they will never be drunk with wine or with beer, yet they are drunkards in this sense, they are drunk with affections for other things in this life. A man may be intoxicated with sorrow, says the Prophet, "Thou shalt be filled with drunkenness, and with sorrow," Ezekiel 23:33. That is, you shall be filled with sorrow until you are drunk with it again. So, a man may be intoxicated with fear, "Drink and be drunken, spew and fall, and rise no more, because of the sword which I will send among you," Jeremiah 25:27. That is, you shall be drunk and stagger to and fro with fear. A man may be intoxicated with delights and with pleasures, and intoxicated with security: they are intoxicated, but not with wine, for the Lord has poured out upon them the spirit of a deep sleep, Isaiah 29:9, 10. That is, you are so secure, and so fast asleep in your lusts, as if you were dead drunk with security. Thus all the affections may be intoxicated with the things of this life. And therefore if ever we would have our affections to be right, let us be sober in all things of the world. You desire food and raiment, then limit your affections with sobriety, and be content. You love the world for the use that you have of it, then limit your affections with sobriety, and use it as if you used it not. Buy as if you bought not, go to the Markets and your Fairs, as if you went not. Sow, reap, and gather in, as if you did it not. And if you need to be merry and jest harmlessly now and then, be marvellously sparing and sober. Eating must be, drinking must be, sleeping must be, and providing for yourselves and your family must be: if ever you love your own souls and salvation, be sparing and sober in these things, lest excess of affections step in in a moment: the devil is always seeking opportunities to deceive you; he is ever like a roaring Lion seeking by all means to devour you. Be sober then and vigilant, for your adversary the devil walketh about seeking whom he may devour, 1 Peter 5:8. When a man is to fight with a stout enemy, will he go and make himself drunk, so that his enemy may attack him when he is drunk? You need to be sober, if it is to fight with the devil; if ever you are even slightly overtaken, even slightly dizzy, then is the devil most active. Temperance and sobriety have a very good name in the Greek tongue, the Spirit of God calls it ἐγκράτεια, that is, the keeper of the mind safe, or the keeper of a man in his wits. Do so, otherwise you shall never be able to set your affections on God. This is an admirable means to keep our affections in tune, to be sober in all things: to be sober-minded, and sober-hearted, and sober-mouthed, and sober-meated, and sober-clothed, and sober-employed. This is the fifth means to set our affections on God, To be sober in all things.

The sixth is this: when we see how apt our affections are to fly out upon vanity, to clip their wings of much of their lawful liberty; not only to abstain from things that are evil and unlawful, but also to abstain from many things that are lawful. There are a thousand lawful things that your heart does desire, which if you do not restrain yourself from, you shall never be able to set your affections upon God. This rule Socrates the very Heathen observed; no man can be safe from falling into unlawful things, but only this man, says he, that abstains from many things that are lawful. It is lawful to drink strong drink, but for you who are apt to over-desire it, it is dangerous. It is lawful to dress finely; but for you who are apt to be proud of it, it is not safe to go to the utmost of what is lawful. If you use the utmost of a thing that is lawful, one step further is unlawful. It is not wise to go to the utmost ridges of a rock, just at the brow of a high cliff; though the ground you walk on may be secure, yet your going is not secure: how soon may you slip with your foot? How soon may dizziness in the head come upon you, and then you break your neck? Perhaps you may go steadily, yes, but perhaps not, but topple down suddenly and be dashed to pieces. It was lawful for Dinah to go forth and see the daughters of the land, but thus she fell to be ravished and used like a whore, Genesis 34:1. It was lawful for Jehoshaphat to visit King Ahab, but his using this lawful visitation drew him to partake in some measure of his sins. It was lawful for Daniel to eat the portion of meat that the King gave him, but he would not, Daniel 1:8. That very lawful thing, if he had used it, would have defiled him. "All these things are lawful for me," you say, "yes, but all these things are not expedient;" because if you take your liberty in all things that are lawful, you will quickly be a slave to your lusts, and under the power of inordinate affections. "All things are lawful for me," says the Corinthian, "yes, but I will not be brought under the power of any," says S. Paul, 1 Corinthians 6:12. As if he had said, all things of this nature are lawful, but I count it not expedient to use them for all that: why? Because if I should take liberty in this kind, I should be brought under the power of my sinful affections. Cavendi sunt affectus, ne illius nos ipsos subjiciamus, says Peter Martyr, Take heed of your affections, they will instantly enslave you. Follow not your pleasure so much as you may, nor your profits and earthly employments so much as you may; drink not, and sleep not, and jest not so much as you may, for if you do, your affections will be caught ere you are aware. Many men and women, they will be enquiring and questioning, what? Is not this lawful? And is not this lawful? Is it not lawful to have a little recreation every day? Is it not lawful to be merry, and to tell a merry tale, and to break a jest now and then? Is it not lawful to sell ale, and keep a victualling house? Is it not lawful to wear such a trinket? Or to style one's hair after such or such a fashion? These questions sound like the speeches of fools that are likely to be deceived in their affections by Satan. For what though they be lawful? I do not deny they are lawful; but the question is this, Are they safe and expedient for you, when your affections are sure to be needlessly excited by these things? O do not needlessly endanger your affections, if ever you may remedy it, "ἐγκράτεια" (egkrateia), says Chrysostom. Look you do not become a slave of your affections: your affections itch after this and that, look you do curb them: if you do not curb them from many things that are lawful, you will never be able to set them upon God. This is the sixth means to set our affections on God, to clip their wings from flying upon the things here below.

The seventh is this, to be abundant in the exercises of godliness. We must be abundant in prayer, and in all other exercises of godliness. When Paul had exhorted good Timothy to be exercised in godliness, 1 Tim. 4:7. in the next verse, he gives him a reason why he so exhorts him. Because, says he, godliness is profitable unto all things, If godliness be profitable for all things, then certainly it's profitable for this, to set our affections upon God. Abound then in good duties, abound in good conference, abound in good and gracious acquaintance, abound in godly meditations. This was David's means whereby his affections came to be earnest upon God. O how I love thy Law, it is my meditation continually! Psal. 119:97. his affections were even wrapped up in his God, O how love I thy Law! He was not able to express how his affections were wrapped. O how love I thy Law! How came they to be so? The reason was this, He was abundant in godly meditations; It is my meditation continually, Abundance in anything, causes the affections to abound. The voluptuous man is abundant in his pleasures, he abounds with his hunting, and hawking, and gaming, and merriments, and therefore his affections are abundantly set hereupon. The covetous man his mind abounds in thinking of the world, his memory abounds with remembering the things of the world, his tongue abounds in talking of such matters, his labours and his cares abound in this kind, and therefore his affections are abundantly set upon these things. There is nothing makes the affections so excessive as abundance, Abound then in the exercises of God's worship, if thou wouldst have thine affections to be abundant that way. Never think thou canst pray enough; hear enough, speak holily enough, examine thy soul enough, nor sanctify the Sabbath enough, never think thou canst reform enough, or do any duty enough. Men serve God as little as they dare, they pray and hold out in their prayers as little as they dare, they show themselves for God as little as they dare, these men's affections can never be upon God, because they love not to be abundant in good duties: thy heart is a great deep, Psa. 64:6. It is not a little winding, or a little turning will fetch up a Bucket out of a deep Well. So the heart I say is a great deep, a little praying, and a little hearing, and a little amending will not fetch up the affections from this great deep unto God, no, Thou must be abundant in goodness and in the duties of goodness, if thou wouldst have thine affections set upon God; provided always that thy heart be renewed and quickened, otherwise abundance will cloy thee. The more thou prayest, the less affections thou wilt have: the more thou hearest, and the more thou speakest of Religion or of grace, the more formal thou wilt be, thine affections will be less set hereupon. O my brethren, this is a cursed crasis and disposition of soul, to be spiritually cloyed in this manner; abound and abound right, else it's too small purpose; if thou abound in good duties, and abound right, this will set their affections upon God. Abound in a thing, and be the thing never so bad, it will soon command thine affections. Let a man be abundant in playing, drinking, or abundant though it be but in the taking of hot waters, I have known some their affections were so to it, that it killed them. Beloved, abound then in good duties, this will take off thine affections from the world, and set them on God. This is the seventh means, to set our affections on God, to be abundant in the duties of holiness.

The eighth is this, Labour to dive down to the bottom of thine affections: the sweetest is at bottom as we say. So the affections that are sweetest to the heart are at bottom. And therefore dive down to the bottom and get up the bottom of thine affections, and set them upon God; thine affections are never set upon God, till them at the bottom are set upon God. A man may set the shallow of his affections upon God, when the bottom is set upon the things of the world. There is many a close hypocrite, he thinks his affections to the world are now dead; but they are not dead; the Fox seems often to be dead, to seize the more cunningly on his prey. So the affections will seem to be dead to the world, that so they may be the more cunning to feed upon the things of the world; they seem to be dead, that is, the shallow of them seems so, but the bottom still is alive to the world, that is not set upon God. Beloved, a man may set the shallow of his affections upon a thing, which the bottom of his affections doth hate. See this in Ammon, his affections were to Tamar, and he loved her. O he would seem to be sick for her. Ay, the shallow of his affections were to her, but anon, out comes the bottom: when the bottom of his affections once did come out, then he did hate her. He hated her worse then he loved her, 2 Sam. 13 15. dive down then to the bottom of thine affections, and labour with all might to get up the bottom, and set them upon God. Here's a man, he hath good affections to repentance and amendment, good affections to be godly and have grace; he reforms much, and he professes much; you would wonder to see this man a year hence to persecute the Minister, and to oppose God's people and make a mock of the power of Religion: but this you may see, if the bottom of his affections be not got up and set upon God. Get up the bottom, and set that upon God, or it is nothing.

There are three means to get up the bottom of thine affections and set them upon God.

First. Be humbled after all thy turning unto God; this will get up the bottom of thine affections to God. A wicked man, before he is turned unto God, may be humbled; as Ahab, Judas, Pharaoh, and many other sinners were humbled before they turned from their sins. When once they have turned from their profaneness and impieties, then they begin to think well of themselves; now they are well, they think. Indeed, before ever they are turned, they may be humbled. Thus, a drunkard, a whoremonger, a mocker, and a profane person may be humbled; their consciences may pull them by the throat as long as they live in these sins, and then their affections are stirred exceedingly. They may weep, sigh, groan, tremble, and be ashamed of their doings; they may be humbled thus before they are turned. But when they are turned from these sins, then they begin to be quiet, secure, and to hope well. Alas! Alas! The bottom is not up yet. But if thou wouldst get up the bottom of thine affections, be humbled after all thy turnings to God. So it was with good Ephraim: "Surely after that I was turned, I repented; and after that I was instructed, I smote upon my thigh, I was ashamed, yea, even confounded" (Jer. 31:19). Ephraim was humbled after he was turned. It was not before he was turned, but after he was turned, he repented and was humbled. This got up the very bottom of his affections unto God. See how full of affections he was. He smote upon his thigh, he was in a holy rage at his own soul, he blushed, he was ashamed, yea, he was even smitten with confusion of face before God. All the bottom of his affections was up; his zeal, his sorrow, his shame, and the whole bottom of all came up then because he was thus humbled.

Secondly, Keep no close lust, no corruption in secret unmortified. As this is a means to get up all the bottom of our affections and set them upon God, so it is a sign too whether we do so or not. For when a man is willing to be searched, who may have been suspected of stealing, if he is willing to be searched, to have his pockets, house, coffers, and all his haunts searched, and he says, "Search me, I have it not," it is a sign he has not stolen it. So it was with the Psalmist. Having said that his affections were set upon God and against those who were against God, he bids God search him and see if he could find that it was contrary. "Search me, O God, and know my heart," or as some translations have it, "and try the ground or the bottom of my heart; see if there be any way of wickedness in me" (Psalms 139:23-24). As if he had said, "If I have any secret corruption that I favor myself in, I confess the bottom of mine affections is rotten; but I am willing to be searched. Search me, O God, and try the ground or the bottom of my heart, and see if it be not so as I profess it to be." I say, as this is a means, so it is a sign too. It is a means to get up the bottom of the affections and set them upon God. For as long as a man has any secret lust, any bottom corruption which he favors himself in, he can never set the bottom of his affections upon God.

Thirdly, consider this: God will shame thee one day if the bottom be not sound. Thou mayest have good affections for a while and be held in high regard as a very good Christian and a fervent believer. But if thine affections are not solid and sound at the bottom, God will shame thee. Though the apple looks very appealing, if it is not sound at the core, it will eventually be revealed. Similarly, though the egg appears lovely, if it is rotten within, it will eventually be evident. God will unmask thee one day and make it clear that thine affections were never right at the bottom. David used this as a means to provoke himself to cultivate a sound heart at the bottom. "Let my heart be sound in thy statutes, that I be not ashamed" (Psalm 119.80). He was loath to experience the shame that would inevitably come if he were not sound at the bottom. Therefore, he pleaded with God that his heart might be sound in His statutes. He was not content with merely having good affections; he sought to have sound and solid affections that would be steadfast at the bottom. "That I be not ashamed," says he. What a shame it will be to see thee condemned at Christ's left hand when thou art now esteemed a good Christian! If thou art not right at the bottom, this will be thy fate.

Let me share with you an experience of my own. I once said to a gentleman who was deeply affected by the Word and professed great love for my ministry, pledging to defend it and hold the Word in high regard, "There are many who seem very eager to approve of the Word and to defend it, but when the Word confronts their bosom sins and gives them no rest in their consciences, I fear they will turn against the minister, the Word, and all before long." "Oh no, God forbid," he replied, "I would be unworthy to live if I were to do so." "Well, well," said I, "I pray God it may not be as I say; but mark my words, and perhaps you shall see it with your own eyes." Within a fortnight, this gentleman, who initially appeared to be such a friend when I first came to the parish, encountered a sermon that reproved and condemned his sin (a sin I never imagined he was guilty of) from the pulpit. From that day forward, he avoided me and opposed me as long as I stayed there. His affections were affected, but they were not sound at the bottom, and therefore he came to this shame. May God have humbled him by now if he is still alive.

It is a good moral rule: "The affections will falsely submit to reason." This holds true in theology as well; the affections will seem to submit to grace when they do not. For as long as the bottom is not sound, they cannot be truly set upon God. They are nothing but flashes, like puddles of water after a shower that quickly dry up. This is the eighth means to set our affections on God: to cultivate a sound foundation for our affections and set them on God.

Beloved, these are the means by which you may set your affections on God. Now, consider how closely it concerns you to use all these means and to conscientiously fulfill this duty. This will become apparent if you consider these two things.

Firstly, the affections are the bonds of the soul, by which it is firmly bound unto sin. You can never repent nor be saved as long as your affections are not turned. Can a prisoner walk when firmly bound in stocks? Your earthly and carnal affections securely bind you in sin; if these bonds are not broken, you can never approach God. When Peter perceived a carnal affection in Simon Magus the Sorcerer, he immediately told him, "I perceive thou art in the gall of bitterness, and in the bond of iniquity" (Acts 8:23). He does not merely say "in iniquity" but also "in the bond of iniquity"; for his carnal affection was a bond, and he was firmly bound in his sins. The Prophet preaches hell and damnation against such men and women; for how can they escape when they are bound and tied to their pleasures and the things of the world? "Woe unto them that draw iniquity with cords of vanity, and sin as it were with a cart-rope" (Isaiah 2:18). Just as great carts are drawn by cart-ropes, so a man's sins are drawn to him by these cords. Chrysostom explains these words to mean both their sins and their woes; they draw both upon themselves. The cords of our affections are the heart's ties to sin; they bind the soul to sin so tightly that it cannot break free. "Woe is to them," says the Lord. Are the affections all like bonds, cords, and cart-ropes, tying the heart to sin? What a woeful state you are in until your affections are set right!

Whatever you tie them to, you draw after you; if you fasten them to the things of this life, you draw them after you; if you fasten them to grace, Christ, and His Word, you pull them after you. "Never was Samson so fast bound with Delilah's withs as he was with his affections to Delilah," says Gregory. Ah, poor enslaved soul, you are in the Devil's stocks; as long as your affections are not rightly fastened, you are heart-bound, soul-bound, and conscience-bound; you are securely bound in his cage. Therefore, it greatly concerns you all to set your affections upon God if you ever desire to flee from the vengeance to come; therefore, use all these means with all conscientiousness to set your affections on God.

Secondly, earthly affections are the preoccupations of the heart; the heart is already preoccupied with the things of this life and is biased against things above. Therefore, there is no hope to persuade you as long as your affections are set upon earthly things. When our Saviour Christ perceived how the Pharisees' affections pursued credit and honour from men, being preoccupied with the desire for human applause, he plainly told them they could never believe or seek the honour of God. "Ye cannot believe," says he; "how can ye believe which receive honour one of another, and seek not the honour that cometh from God only?" (John 5:44). It is grievous to be prejudiced and preoccupied with any good other than God. It is a futile endeavour to reason with a prejudiced person; they will not yield, no matter what. As long as our affections are set on the world, our hearts are prejudiced. Therefore, until we follow the prescribed means to set our affections right, we cannot hope to convert you or to bring any good to your souls.

The Seventh Sermon

"Set your affections on things that are above, and not on things which are on the earth." – Colossians 3:2

Are the affections the motions of the heart, and must we set them on God? This may teach us one lesson by the way; we that are God's Ministers must take notice from hence how to qualify our preaching, namely, to stir up the affections of men's hearts. Every man, says Rodolphus Agricola, that hath any learning at all, is able to teach; but to shake men's affections, and turn men's hearts, he is an extraordinary man that can do this: after this manner was the preaching of our Saviour, he did so move the affections of his hearers, that the Text says, they were astonished at his doctrine, Matthew 7:28. Why so? The Evangelist makes answer in the next verse, for he taught them as one having authority, and not as the Scribes: that is, not so cold as the Pharisees. He was not such a frigid and cold Teacher as the Pharisees and Scribes were; the people sat like immovable stocks in their seats when the Scribes were teaching; they were not moved a jot. But our Saviour was a powerful Teacher; he taught them as one having authority, and not as the Scribes: his

Sermons were moving and forceable. John the Baptist wrought strongly on the affections of his Auditors; they could not possibly hold but cried outright as they heard him. The people asked him, "What shall we do?" The Publicans cried out, "Master, what shall we do?" The Soldiers also, whose affections are as hard to be moved as any, yet they cried out too, "And what shall we do?" Luke 3:14. This use is plainly grounded on my Text. God's Ministers, you know, are God's Instruments to bring men to faith and repentance, and reconcile them to God: and therefore, if this be your duty, to set your affections on God, we must labour to work on your affections to provoke you to do it. The reasons for it are these.

Firstly, because the Word is full of affections; full of affections of love to woo a man to God, full of affections of pity to yearn upon men in their misery, full of affections of terror to terrify the wicked; and therefore, that Minister who preaches not affectionately, preaches but one half of the Word, he preaches but the dead corpse of the Truth, as I may call it: he does not preach the life and the soul of the truth. The affections of a speech are the soul of a speech; both make up the whole of the Word. "Is not my Word like unto fire, and like a hammer that breaketh the rocks in pieces?" Jeremiah 23:29. If the Word be a fire, he who delivers it coldly, delivers the Word otherwise than it is. Would you not say that a man were ridiculous who, when his neighbour's house is on fire, should go and coldly advise the Parish in this manner; "Oh my dear neighbours, you should do well to look to your houses, lest fire fall upon them, as now of late I understood it hath done; I pray let me persuade you to provide water, otherwise all your goods and mine too will be consumed to ashes." It is true that this man says; but would not men deem him a fool? The truth is the truth of affection, and he leaves out the affection of the truth. Nature hath taught us another course in such a case. He would run crying into the street, "Fire, fire, help, help, for the Lord's sake; water, water, in all haste, alas, alas, we are undone, quickly, speedily, run for ladders; pull down this rafter here, cut down that beam there, unthatch the house, what mean you? Stir hands, arms, legs, hie thee for water, run thee for iron crooks, crows, hooks, buckets, haste, haste; we are all undone." Here now is the affection of the truth: the like must a Minister do, who knowing his people wallow in sin, in the state of hell and damnation, as many as go on in their courses, he ought not with filed phrases and mellow-mouthed words, nor with cold exhortations admonish his hearers, but he must put in the affection of the Word in his Sermons: he must cry "fire, fire, the fire of hell is among you, the fire is kindled, sin is entered into the soul: Oh the water of tears, tears, repentance, repentance, help yourselves for God's sake: the devil stands ready to devour you, death watches unawares to strike you, hell-mouth gapeth to swallow you; look about you, stir yourselves and consider, or ye perish in a moment. Leave off your riots, down with your pleasures, away with your vanities, put on Christ quickly, work out your salvation with fear and trembling. See ye not men die daily before you on a sudden, falling to hell, haste, haste, flatter not your souls, time is uncertain, the danger is too certain, the punishment eternal, damnation is intolerable." Thus must a Minister preach this truth. It is a truth full of affection; the affection must be delivered as well as the body of the truth. "All the imaginations of the thoughts of man's heart are only evil," Genesis 6:5. As this is a truth, so there is a great deal of affection in this truth, the affection of loathing. Do we think when the Lord said it, he said it coldly and nakedly; "all the imaginations, etc."? No, he said it with a great deal of affection, of loathing, etc. "Oh Jerusalem, Jerusalem, etc. Oh that thou hadst known, etc." As this is a truth, so there is a great deal of affection in this truth, affection of pity. There is a great deal of affection in every threatening, a great deal of affection in every command, a great deal of affection in every promise, in every truth. Christ does not bid us preach the letters, and syllables, and propositions of his Word, but his Word. "Now my Word is like fire," says God; "fire is the stirringest element of all elements, and therefore if there be any feeling at all in you, the Word is able to stir you, even as if ye had a fire in your bowels." Beloved, either we that are God's Ministers are unskilful to handle the Word, or else ye are senseless and stupid, if ye do not sit upon hot coals for to hear it: it will make the drunkard's heart ache to hear what this Word says to him: it will make the worldling's heart ache, and the secure Christian's heart ache. The Word is fire, "Did not our hearts burn within us, while he opened to us the Scriptures?" Luke 24:32. The Word did so inflame their affections, that their hearts burned to hear it. Does not the godly heart burn to hear the sweetness of God's promises? And burn when the Scriptures are opened to direct thee? And so on the other side, does not the Usurer's heart burn, when the Scriptures are opened that rip up his sins? Does not the carnal professor's heart burn now and then as he sits, when the Scriptures are opened to show him his rottenness? There be such scorching texts in the Word; texts of death, texts of judgment, texts of hell and damnation; they may well make a wicked heart burn to hear them; and therefore, the Word being so full of affection, a Minister who preaches it must needs be an affectionate preacher, if he be a true preacher; otherwise, he does not preach the whole Word.

Secondly, as the Word is full of affection itself, so it seems that a man should be full of affection that obeys it. God loves no other obedience but obedience with affection; he loves a cheerful giver (2 Corinthians 9:7). So, God loves a cheerful obeyer, a cheerful repenter, a cheerful believer; whatever we do in his service, he loves we should do it with affection. Should a Minister preach without any affection, perhaps he may reason men out of many of their sins and prevail with them to take up the duties of religion, but all would be formality, without any affection. It is a good saying of Augustine, the godly must have affections in obedience, otherwise they are not obedient.

There are two things in every Commandment of God.

First, the duty commanded to be done, "Fear God and keep his Commandments." This is the whole duty (Ecclesiastes 12:13). That is, there is never a duty that a man has commanded him but it is within the compass of the Commandments of God. So that in every Commandment, there is a duty.

Secondly, the strength of affection wherein the Commander commands it, and therefore the Commandment is called God's will. "Teach me to do thy will, O God," (Psalm 143:10). It is called God's pleasure, "Bless the Lord, ye Ministers of his, that do his pleasure," (Psalm 103:21). It is called God's desire, "Thou desiredst truth in the inward parts," (Psalm 51:6), because the strength of God's will and desire, and pleasure, and affection lies in it. These two things being in every Commandment of God, it follows of necessity that a man must have his affections in obedience, otherwise, he is not obedient. As God does not only command me, but also with affection he commands me: so I must not only do the thing he commands, but with all affection I must do it, or else I never obey him. "Virtuti immitte furorem," says Homer, Add affections to thy virtue, virtue is no virtue without the affections; prayer is no prayer without thine affections be in it, repentance is no repentance without thine affections be in it. Whatever duty thou dost, if thou dost it not with all thine affections, it is abomination to God: and therefore, the Minister that preaches must stir up affections: if he does not stir up affections, the religion he begets in the hearts of his hearers is likely to be little better than wretched formality.

Thirdly, as the Word is full of affection itself, and requires affection in them that obey it, so men are very dull in affection to embrace it; they are dull of hearing (Hebrews 5:11). They have dull ears, and dull hearts, and dull affections: tell them they shall perish because they do not repent; they will be damned because they will not obey: they shall be saved that will; they are like Gallio, they care for none of these things; and therefore now we that are Ministers must strive to make them hear whether they will or no. "Cry aloud," says God, "spare not, lift up thy voice like a trumpet, show my people their transgressions," (Isaiah 58:1). Do not only say a Sermon to them, but cry it: nor only so, but cry aloud, they are deaf: spare not, thou wilt never stir them if thou sparest. Spare not, spare neither rich nor poor, neither great nor small, lift up thy voice like a trumpet, that is, preach so, that if it be possible, thou mayst move their affections. It is a similitude taken from the Trumpet in battle, though the Soldier be faint-hearted, it will stir him up with affection to fight. Great Alexander was so stirred up at the trumpeting of one Antigenidas, an admirable trumpeter, that all his courageous affections were up, and his fingers did itch to be fighting. So lift up thy voice like a trumpet, stir them up, if by any means thou canst. Oh, they are very dull and senseless, and hard to be affected, and therefore we must study how to work on their affections.

If you ask me how must the Minister stir up affections? I answer.

First, Negatively, not with the enticing words of man's wisdom (1 Corinthians 2:4). Some men indeed out of these words do gather that Saint Paul condemned all eloquence and affectionate preaching. But this cannot be, that he should condemn that which he most shown himself, most of all the Apostles of Christ. He was such an eloquent golden-mouthed man that the Lycaonians thought he had been another Mercury; he was such a sweet speaker (Acts 14:12). He was such an affectionate Orator that he made Agrippa's bowels even yearn to be a Christian, and Felix to tremble. Saint Augustine conceived him to be gifted with such an admirable power this way of Almighty God that it was one of his three wishes, if he might have it for wishing; namely, to hear Saint Paul preach in a Pulpit; and therefore he does not condemn all affectionate and eloquent preaching; but he condemns that flattering kind of affected Rhetoric, whereby men that preached themselves, tickled men's ears, and delighted them with luscious phrases of Oratory; handling such points as might please the fantasies of their hearts, rather than to convince them of their sins: thinking it too precise, too base to preach of men's damnable estate and condition in sin, the curse of the Law that all men are under till they be new creatures in Christ; the taking up of Christ's Cross: to be hated, and mocked, and persecuted of all men, for Christ's sake and his Gospel. These points, they either thought to be too rustic, and burly, and austere, or they sugared them over with their comments, and tickled the people with more velvet-like passages of mercy. I say, this kind of eloquence, and this kind of preaching, with the enticing words of man's wisdom, does the Apostle condemn, and therefore I do not mean this. How then must a Minister stir up affections? I answer, he must stir up affections five ways.

First, By preaching to the life, As a Painter then paints a man well, when he paints him to the life; he paints it so to the life, as if it were a living man indeed. So then does a Preacher preach affectionately when he preaches to the life; when he preaches of hell, he preaches to the life, as if hell were before men's eyes; when he preaches of heaven, as if the people did see it with their eyes as it were. As King James said of a good preacher in this Kingdom; this Preacher, says he, preaches as if death were at my back: so a good Preacher preaches to the wicked, as if vengeance were at their backs, as if hell were at their backs; he preaches to the godly as if Christ were at their backs, and heaven at their backs. If this kind of preaching will not work on men's affections, their affections are bewitched, "O foolish Galatians, who hath bewitched you, that ye should not obey the truth, before whose eyes Jesus Christ hath been evidently set forth, crucified among you?" (Galatians 3:1). Paul among them had preached Christ to the life; so evidently, and so plainly, had he preached Christ crucified, as if they had seen him crucified before their eyes. Certainly, thought he, these people's affections are bewitched, that are no better wrought on. When Galba would persuade the Spaniards against Nero for his cruelty, he set out so visibly his cruelty, that they might even see it with their eyes. Lycurgus so expressed the difference of good education and of bad, that the people might even see it with their eyes. Not as though preachers should do as they did, or as some that I have read of, have done; who brought a dead skull into the pulpit, that the people might see death even with their eyes. We have no such warrant in Scripture; but they must do it with the lively teaching of the truth. And therefore the Apostle says, that true preaching is in the demonstration of the spirit (1 Corinthians 2:4). When the truth is demonstrated with evidence.

Secondly, By being full of affections himself: Affection in the speaker is likely to beget affection in the hearer. "It cannot be otherwise," says Cicero. Cicero, being an excellent spokesman, whenever he pleaded before the people of Rome, to beget any affections in them, he would be sure to put on those affections himself. If he would move them to grief, he would be full of the affection of grief. When to pity, he would be full of affections of pity; when to anger, his countenance would be full of anger. "The highest point of moving the affections in another is to be endued with those affections thyself," says Quintilian. It is an old maxim in Oratory, and in all moving of the affections of others, "Pectus est quod facit disertos." It is a man's own breast that makes him be affectionate and eloquent. If a man's own breast is piteous, and full of compassion and bowels, that man is an eloquent persuader to pity. If a man's own breast is loving, and kind, and full of affections, that man is an eloquent speaker to move love: "Si vis me flere, dolendum primum ipse tibi," If thou wouldst have me weep, weep thyself first. "What mean you to weep and break my heart," says the Apostle (Acts 21:13), it burst his very heart to see others stand weeping about him. There are many clamorous Preachers, says Calvin, who declaim against the sins of the people and thunder against the iniquities of their Parish, and make as though they had a great deal of zeal, that never move a jot; the affections of the people are not stirred up a whit; because the people see plainly, through all their actings and vehement enforcements, that such Ministers are not affected themselves, but only exercise their sides and their throat, as if they would act it on a stage. But O, says he, labor to mourn for their sins in thine heart, before thou labor to move them. Be thou more affected thyself, than thou undertakest to affect them. Saint Paul did so move the affections of Dionysius and Damaris, and others at Athens, that the Text says, they clave to Saint Paul. Certain men clave to him and believed (Acts 17:34). He preached so movingly, that their affections did even cleave to him as he preached. How came it about that he stirred up affections in them? Look into the 16th verse, and there you shall see he was greatly affected himself. "His spirit was stirred in him," says Saint Luke, "when he saw the city wholly given to idolatry." He could not have stirred up affections in them if he had not been filled with affections himself. O beloved, our hearts are grievously straitened, and our souls are woefully stopped, that we are not more affected ourselves at your miseries than we be: would it not fetch tears from our eyes, and groans from our bowels, to see how desperately ye are hardened, but that we are too little affected ourselves?

You know the damned abuses in your Parish, the cursed sins that reign in your houses, and the stupid security ye are in, yet nothing can move you. Your consciences cannot be ignorant ye are carnal, and are not yet Saints, nor born again many of you; your consciences can tell you ye are Saints, or else ye are hell-hounds, and if ye die as ye are, ye have no evidence for heaven, but ye may be damned ere long for all that ye know. Ye can hear this every time ye go to Church, and yet no reformation, no show of humiliation, no show of grace nor repentance nor anything; "What weeping Simonides can weep sufficiently for these things?" Paul, knowing some abuses among the Corinthians, that many of them were likely to be damned forever, out of much affliction and anguish of heart, says he, "I wrote unto you with many tears" (2 Corinthians 3:4), "pene quot syllabas, tot lacrymas," as Haymo speaks, that is, he shed as many tears as he wrote syllables, he could hardly write for wetting the paper with tears which he wrote on. O that we who are God's Ministers could be so affected! The Lord lay it not to our charge that we are not: but O that our heads were water, and our eyes were a fountain of tears, that we might weep day and night for these things. Ye think your souls are safe, alas! We know they are desperate. We know that your drunkenness will damn you, and your swearing and lying and company-keeping will undo you. We know your pride and your hardness of heart are symptoms and infallible marks of such as are yet no better than reprobates. Ye hope your crying God mercies will help you, we know they cannot. Ye hope that God's mercies will relieve, we know they will not, unless ye be new creatures. Ye trust God will not be so strict as we say, we know he will. Ye imagine ye are not led by the devil, though ye sin thus and thus, we know ye be, and the devil the God of this world rules in your minds and your consciences. Neither are ye able, unless ye be Atheists and devils incarnate, to deny God to be God, and his Scripture to be Scripture, ye are not able to deny it. O that we would sigh, and sob, and groan in our pulpits. O that we could even wet our cushions with tears, and yearn over your souls as we preach; I beseech you consider, will you never believe nor be affected till ye feel it? Lord, when thy hand is lifted up they will not see, but they shall see and be ashamed, and the fire shall devour them (Isaiah 26:11), "I protest unto you, I could find in my heart to fall down on my knees to every one of you all, were it profitable to beseech you to consider this, now God's hand is lifted up, and he calls to you and ye will not hear, he shows you your sins, and ye will not see, you shall see," says he, "and be ashamed, and the fire of hell shall devour you." Take heed ye see not too late. O that ye had known at least in this thy day, before they be hid from thine eyes. God will hide his grace from thine eyes, and his spirit from thy heart, if nothing can move thee. I pray God affect our hearts with these things, that we who are your Ministers may be more touched ourselves. This is the second means whereby we might move you if we were affected ourselves.

Thirdly, By being godly ourselves. As we must be affected ourselves, so if ever we mean to stir up affections in the heart, we must be godly ourselves. Aristotle requires this in an Orator, that he be a good man, "ἀγαθὸς καὶ σώφρων", the good manners and the life of the speaker have the greatest power to persuade the affections. Hence is that usual saying of the vulgar. "He that preaches well, and lives ill, pulls that down with one hand which he built with the other." Nay, commonly a man loathes a good saying out of a foul mouth. Let a drunken Minister exhort to sobriety, for the most part the people do loathe it. Let an adulterous or covetous Minister exhort to be godly and religious, for the most part they abhor it. Let a loose Minister preach of strictness of life and conversation, and zeal and purity, Solomon says it is like a lame man's legs when one is shorter than the other (Proverbs 26:7), that is an ill sight: A wicked

Minister can never stir up the affections of the people aright. Gregory Nazianzen would have a Minister "ἢ μὴ κηρύττειν ἢ καλῶς βιοῦντα", Either not preach at all, or preach by a good and godly life. Otherwise, the people will have little affection to hear him: nay, which is lamentable, it is usual in the world, not only to set their affections against a wicked Minister's preaching but also to loathe the very ordinance itself: when Eli his sons were wicked, and sons of Belial, the Text says, the people loathed God's offerings. "The sin of the young men was very great before the Lord, for men abhorred the offering of the Lord" (1 Samuel 2:17). At the best, the people, though never so greedy otherwise to hear, yet if the Minister do not as he says, they have small affection to hear him: Christ knew this by his Disciples, who were willing to hear him whenever he preached, but he knew they had little affection to hear a Sermon of the Pharisees, who said and did not. And therefore he was fain to command them not to be offended at that, but to hear them. It was not then in vain that the Apostle exhorts Titus to look to his own life. "In all things show thyself a pattern," says he, "a pattern of good works." For if the Minister that preaches be not a good pattern to his people, his Sermons will not be so able to stir up affections in their hearts. "Pasce verbo, pasce exemplo," says Gregory: we must feed them by doctrine and feed by our example: this is the way to stir up affections in our hearers. It is true, the people ought to be stirred up by the Word, in whose mouthsoever it be, and it is their fault that they be not, but yet it will never be so: the Minister's contrary life in any particular, as it is cursed of God, so likewise it is a scandalous thing unto others, and an infinite occasion of offence, and takes off the edge of the Word. Yea, commonly it does more hurt than all the preaching can do good. For thus men will argue, "If it be necessary to live as he says, then why does not he live so himself? He hath more learning than I," and the like: nay, they call the Word into question, and hoodwink their souls with presumptuous pretences. Thus millions of souls are gone to hell with their Minister for company: "Malus Minister est nisus Diaboli," It is a true saying of a Father, "An evil Minister is the devil's Gos-Hawk or Sparrow-Hawk. He goes a birding for hell." But why speak I of these things among you whom it concerneth not? Yea, it concerns you much every way. For as it is a curse to a Parish that a Minister is wicked, so is the Parish tied as ever they love their own souls, to pray unto God that he would sanctify their Minister more and more, that the Word may run and be glorified, for the life of the Minister hath a great hand in moving the affections. The holiest Ministers move most.

Fourthly, By the due carriage of their voices, when the Minister is affected himself: I do not say it is always so, for some have not the same command of themselves through accidental reasons: but commonly when the Minister is affected himself, the inward affections of his own breast dispose the voice into some gracious manner of expressing the same. As Paul that was full of grief and sorrow for the people's sins, he for the most part preached with a weeping voice, "Many walk," says he, "of whom I have told you often, and now again tell I you even weeping, they are enemies of the Cross of Christ, whose end is destruction, &c." (Philippians 3:18, 19). And truly if we consider the iniquities of the times, and the sins of most men, how lamentable their conditions be, no other affection better suits than this. "Loquere flebiliter," says Bucolcerus to a preacher, speak mournfully, and sorrowfully, the very voice itself will somewhat mollify the affections of the people. Certainly, it is an ordinance of God, and very moving, to speak according to the point in hand. To speak compassionately in points of pity, to speak rejoicingly in points of comfort, to speak most terribly in points of terror. As Cato advised that soldiers should terrify their enemies with terrible voices. Neither is it amiss, that when the Minister threatens the judgments of

God against rebellious sinners, he should compose his voice accordingly. "I know not what hidden occult influence the voice hath into the affections," saith S. Augustine, "but a great influence it hath." When a Minister goes dreamingly on, the people sit carelessly and regard it not, and let him say never so good matter, they heed it not; let him threaten, or comfort, or command, or reprove, they respect all alike, for they see no difference in the Minister, I know the people should not do thus, but such is the corruption of men, thus they will do; now God hath given many of his messengers more wakening voices, as petty instruments to provoke men's affections somewhat the more. And truly we are bound to make conscience thereof, that our very voice may be a comment upon our matter; 'twas a pretty story of Demosthenes, when one told him that he was beaten and misused exceedingly by such a companion. It seems he told it so by rote as we say, showing no affection at all in his telling: "Why?" says Demosthenes: "hath he beaten thee? I do not believe he hath beaten he." "No?" says the man: he was much troubled to hear him deny it, and so he spake eagerly and in a chafe, "I am sure he beat me, thus he did, and thus he did, and do you not call this beating?" "Now I believe," says Demosthenes, "I believe now he hath beaten thee indeed, now I hear the voice of a man that was beaten." So if we should dreamingly utter our voice, and reprove our hearers, they scarce believe they are reproved, because they do not hear the voice of a reprover. Let us deliver uses of terror to them, they hardly believe any terror in it, because they do not hear the voice of terror. But when the Minister is affected aright, and his affections direct the carriage of the voice along, the voice itself does more significantly express the matter; and this no question is very moving.

But then let me tell you, if this be it ye look for, and if ye can be carping at a Minister for the want of this, what the Lord accounts of you. He sets it as a brand upon the wicked Jews that they were affected with the

Prophet Ezekiel's pleasant voice when they were affected with little else (Ezekiel 33:32). Even a rare and a worthy Moses may be defective in this case, and woe is the people that findeth fault. But however, be the voice of a godly Minister never so mean, yet there will be ever some hidden grace in it, whereby more or less, it appears unto the consciences of them that have ears to hear. This is the fourth thing whereby a Minister may stir up affections, by the due carriage of his voice.

Fifthly, I might add, by a decent action. For my part, I have little reason to name it, but verily, it is a blessing of Christ to them that have it, for they have a great advantage over the affections of their hearers. Cicero says, some were esteemed viri diserti, eloquent and moving men, but for want of action they could not put their gifts in practice, habiti sunt infantes, they were esteemed infants in this profession, says he. Action we see is much employed in the preaching of the Prophets and the holy men of God. Ezekiel was commanded to stamp with the feet, Isaiah commanded to go naked, Jeremiah commanded to put a yoke on his neck. John the Baptist was tota vox, he was all-voice; the voice of a crier in the wilderness, Mat. 3:3. his eyes spake, and his face spake, his hands spake, and his body spake, yea, his life, and diet, and all spake, he was all-voice. The Prophets stretched forth their hands to the people in fullness of affection. "I have spread forth my hands all the day unto a rebellious people," Isa. 65:2. S. Paul set his eyes upon Elymas the sorcerer, Act. 13:9. "O full of subtlety, and all mischief, thou child of the devil, thou enemy of all righteousness, wilt thou not cease to pervert the right ways of the Lord? The Lord's hand is upon thee, and thou shalt be blind, &c." It is counted a grand sin in old Eli, that he did not frown on his sons, 1 Sam. 3:13. Why does the Text express Eli's not severely threatening his sons, by this action of frowning? But only because they that do severely threaten, do use to frown, Thus ye see how that God's Ministers have used action to move affections.

THE EIGHTH SERMON

"Set your affections on things that are above, and not on things which are on the earth." – Colossians 3:2

Must our affections be set upon God? Then this reproves those who set their affections on the earth. The matter is reducible to four heads.

The first is the multiplicity of the affections; they are very many in number.

The second is the arrangement, or the checker-wise order of the affections. As they are many, so they are intertwined and woven one within another, so that whatever they are set on, they bind the heart to it.

The third is the degree the affections are in, in relation to other acts of the soul.

The fourth is the intensity of the affections, which is zeal. From all these four heads, I will show you the woeful aggravation of this sin: not setting our affections on God.

First, From the multitude and multiplicity of the affections: a man cannot set his affections upon earth, but he must set them all upon earth: the affections they all go together, and are many. Not only four, as Boethius does count them: nor only five, as Galen does reckon them: nor only eleven, as Aristotle does number them: nor only twenty, as Cardan does sum them; but they are like a swarm of Bees, as Laelius Peregrinus does compare them for multitude. Plato says they are innumerable, without question they are many.

Now, what a woeful aggravation is this of this sin, to set thine affections on the earth! Thou settest all thine affections thereon, if thou settest one thou settest all; for they all go together. Like the Angels that sinned, they all fell together, So when the affections fell off from God, they all fell together. Like the two eyes of the body, they both look one way; like the two ears, one doth not hear one sound, and another another. If thou lovest those things that are carnal, it is certain thy desires are all carnal, thy joys, and delights, and thy hopes are all carnal, thy fears, and thy griefs, and thy sorrows are all carnal; if one of them be set on the things here on earth, all are: were there but one affection that way, it were the less; but if thine affections be set upon these things, not one, nor two, nor ten, but numberless multitudes, whole swarms of affections are all earthly. Thou art altogether brutish and foolish, Jer. 10:8. That is, thine affections are altogether brutish and beastly, altogether filthy or stinking, for so the word signifies, Psalms 14:3. That is thine affections are altogether stinking and noisome affections. I proved before, that when the affections are carnal, they all like so many devils do bewitch thee.

O foolish Galatians, who hath bewitched you? It is grievous enough to be plagued with one devil, He must needs run whom the devil drives: one devil will drive thee fast enough to hell. One affection if it were single, will hurry thee fast enough to hell, what then are the whole legions of affections? They are like the legion of devils that entered into the Swine, the herd ran violently down a steep place into the sea, Luke 8:33. They ran with all violence to be drowned, when a legion of devils did drive them. So thou must needs run with all violence down into the lake, when a legion of affections, like a legion of devils doth hurry thee, Sic cuique Deus fit dira cupido, says the Poet. The very heathen man saw this, that every man's evil affection was his devil, and therefore the whole legion of affections are a legion of devils.

Do ye not see how ye are tost up and down all the day long, tan-quam pila diaboli, as the devils tennis-balls, as Odo speaks: from worldly delights unto worldly desires, from desires unto fears, from fears unto melancholies, from melancholies to angers and vexations, from them again unto carnal comforts? These are all like a legion of devils that hurry thee up and down till thou art hurried to hell, &c. If thine affections be carnal, they are a legion of devils to drive thee. It is a merry devil that makes thee so greedy of pleasure and of mirth; a surly devil, that makes thee so choleric and touchy; a giddy devil, that makes thee so fearful and timorous; an unclean devil, that makes thee so desirous of drinking and company-keeping. Anger and wrath is a devil; Let not the soul go down upon thy wrath, neither give place to the devil, Eph. 4:26, 27. That is, do not give way to thy wrath, when thou givest way to thy earthly desires, thou givest way to the devil. When thou givest way to thine earthly delights, and thy sorrow, and thy melancholy, thou givest way to the devil. Look how many earthly affections thou hast that thou givest the way to, so many devils are in thee. Dost thou think thou art a child of God, when thy conscience tells thee, that such and such earthly affections have way in thy heart? Alas! Thou hast a devil. Be sober, for your adversary the devil, 1 Peter 5:8. mark, every giddy affection is a devil, our adversary the devil comes with it. Yea, so many earthly affections, so many devils, and wilt thou set thine affections upon things that are earthly? If thou dost, thou hast a legion of devils within, This is the first head, the multitude and the multiplicity of the affections, the affections are many.

The second head is taken from the stichomythia, or the checkerwise order of the affections. As the affections are many, so look where they are set, there they are platted, and woven, and hampered together. God that first created man upright and good, he gave him affections so to twist and hamper his heart upon good, that it might be the harder to loosen it. He gave him the affection of love to embrace good. If the good were wanting, he gave him the affection of desire, to hunger after it. If the good were possible to get, he gave him the affection of hope to expect it: if the good were once gotten, he gave him the affection of joy to delight in it. If there were any danger to lose it, he gave him the affection of fear to be afraid of it. If the good were once lost indeed, he gave him the affection of grief and of sorrow to lament it. If he should meet with anything that would hinder him in the prosecution of good, he gave him the affection of hatred to oppose it, &c. Thus God embroidered the affections, and wove them together, that still man's heart might be knit by the affections to good and to God.

And wilt thou now set thine affections on the things of this life? Thou little thinkest how thou twistest and hamperest thy soul about these things, thine affections will make thee live and die a carnal wretch. Had not Erasistratus cured Antiochus of his carnal affection, it had cost him his life, for he was sick of it unto death. Galen says, he met with many sick patients, if he had not cured their affections, he had never recovered them. The affections hamper the soul unto death. So if thou set thine affections on the things here on earth, they will so hamper thy heart, that unless thine affections be cured, thy soul is desperately incurable; they entangle thy soul, thou canst not get free.

And therefore S. Peter calls falling into earthly affections, he calls it, entangling. If after they have escaped the pollutions of the flesh they are again entangled, 2 Pet. 2:20. That is, if after they have once gotten out, they fall in again; because they cannot fall in again, but their lusts and affections will not entangle them again. Be not entangled again with the yoke of bondage, Gal. 5:1. Paul knew if the Galatians were addicted to the Ceremonies of the Law, they would affect them more then the Commandments of Christ. And therefore he gives them advice no further to use them, because their hearts would be entangled if they did; No man that warreth, entangleth himself with the affairs of this life, 2 Tim. 2:4. A soldier had not need to have a new married wife, or a new-born child, or a new-purchased ground, a new-planted vineyard, a new suit at Law in the Chancery: Alas! Then his affections would be a gadding, when he should be fighting. O my wife at home, and O my child at home, and I would I might taste of my vineyard at home, and O that I could follow my cause in the Court, this were to entangle him in war, he could not fight valiantly. Thus the affections do entangle a man. So if thine affections be earthy, they will entangle thee, thou canst not be free for the seeking of heaven, or of Christ; thine affections are so complicated and hampered, thou canst be in no place, in no estate nor condition, but some affections or other will entangle thee.

Thou lovest thy land and thy living, and thy things in the world; O how are thine affections entangled, what case soever thou art in? Thine affections lie checker-wise and will have thee. If thou beest rich, the affections of pleasure or delight, or security, there they will have thee. If thou beest poor, the affections of desire and discontent; this thou desirest, and that thou wouldest fain have, there thy wishings, and wouldings and carkings will have thee. If thou beest crossed, or troubled, or afflicted, the affections of grief and of sorrow, and of melancholy, these there will have thee. If thou beest injured, abused, or provoked, which falls out very often, the affections of anger and revenge, these then will have thee. If thou beest in danger of sickness or distress, or loss of this or that, the affections of fear and the like, they lie in ambush to catch thee. If thou comest to the Word, and there thou art told thou art a damned man as long as thou livest as thou dost, the affections of vain hopings and trustings, they lie in scout for to take thee: thus thou art entangled when thine affections are earthy, in what case soever thou art in, they entangle thee. Sometimes thou art merry and jocond for a pang, anon thou art melancholy and sad for a fit. Sometimes thou art angry with a servant, or a child, or a wife, or a neighbor, anon thou art pleased. Sometime a danger comes, and fears thee, anon it is gone, and thou art secure. Sometimes one affection, sometimes another, Sometimes a hating, and sometimes a loving, sometimes desiring, and sometimes hoping. Thus thou livest, and thus thou diest, and perishest forever through the entanglements.

The third head is taken from the degrees the affections are in, in regard to other acts of the soul. And here is a subdivision of heads.

1.   The affections provoke thoughts, and therefore if the affections are earthy, the thoughts are all earthy.

2.   The affections increase lusts, and therefore if the affections are carnal, the lusts are all carnal.

3.   The affections infer purposes and resolutions, and therefore if the affections are to the things of this life, the purposes and resolutions of the heart are so too.

4.   The affections infer devisings and contrivings, and therefore if the affections are vain, so are the devices. From all which you may see the infinite misery you are in if the affections are set here below. First, Because if your affections are set here below, so are your thoughts. When Saul had a treacherous affection towards David, he made as though he did affect him so well as to make him his son-in-law; it was a treacherous affection: but the text says, so were his thoughts. Saul thought to make David fall by the hand of the Philistines, 1 Sam. 18:25. As his affections were treacherous, so his thoughts were in like manner treacherous. The affections are the feet of the soul, as I told you; now when these feet run to evil, so do the thoughts. Their feet run to evil, their thoughts are thoughts of iniquity, Isa. 59:7. So that look what your affections are to, to that are your thoughts. You may remember what was proved to you about the thoughts: if you habitually set your thoughts upon the things in this world, to be thinking of your sports and your pleasures, your apparel, and your fashions, your food, and your drink, your means, and your living; if your thoughts are set hereupon, you are a person who has never repented since you were born; you have yet no part nor interest in Christ, you are yet no better than a damned wretch, heir apparent of hell and everlasting destruction. Thus it is with you, if your thoughts are habitually set thus; but if your affections are set here below, so without question are your thoughts.

Firstly, because if your affections are earthy, so are your thoughts: the affections provoke you to be thinking of such things as you have most mind to. Haman did mightily affect honour, and therefore his thoughts ran upon his honour and promotion. The King had no sooner said,

"What shall be done to the man whom the King delighteth to honour?" but presently his thoughts were agog. Haman thought in his heart, "Whom would the King honour but me?" (Esth. 6:6). When Haman was affected with wrath against Mordecai, instantly such were his thoughts. "He thought scorn," says the text (Esth. 3:6). David, speaking of his enemies that were ill-affected towards him, says that their thoughts were against him, "all their thoughts are against me for evil" (Psalms 56:5). So, if your affections are carnal, your thoughts are carnal, and you cannot think seriously of the good of your soul.

Come and let me think seriously, how do I think to be saved? May not a reprobate pray as well as I pray? Hear the Word as well as I hear it? Believe as well as I believe? Did not wicked Esau, who sought a place for repentance, carefully with tears repent as well as I? Had not cursed Balaam as good intentions as I? He would not, for a houseful of silver and gold, go beyond the commandment of God. Alas! Alas! Your carnal affections will not suffer you to think seriously of your souls. Have you ever thought seriously whether you are a new creature or not? Whether Christ is in you, yes or no? What if I should die now? Have I evidences for Heaven, yes or no? The Scripture says thus and thus, so and so they must live that look to be saved, do I live so? God says, such and such shall be damned, namely, all that live in any known sin; God cannot lie; Is there never a sin I know I live in? Poor woeful soul, your carnal affections have not suffered you to think seriously of these things since you were born. Maybe now and then you have some loose thoughts of some such matters, straggling thoughts, glancing, running thoughts of your soul, and of heaven, and of death, but you never do seriously think of them. No, your earthly affections provoke your thoughts otherwise, your affections have such influence into your thoughts that Macarius calls them affections.

Is not this then a pitiful condition to set our affections here below? To be drawn away from thinking seriously of our souls; they drive you to hell and will not permit you to think seriously whither you go until you are there. O grievous condition! Will a prisoner that is condemned to be hanged tomorrow be thinking how he may get new clothes and a new suit? Will he be thinking how he may purchase? How he may have a good supper? If he is thinking on such things when he shall be hanged tomorrow for all that he knows; he is sure he is condemned, and the gallows is built, and the halter is provided, and if he does not get a pardon, it is certain he shall be executed, and he knows not yet whether ever he shall get it; maybe he may if he seeks hard, if he now is thinking of pleasures and profits, and the like, when his life lies at the stake, you will say, he is woefully affected with these things: and will you be so affected with the things of this life, when you may be in hell tomorrow? You are sure the sentence of damnation is upon you yet, and you shall surely be damned being as you are; will you, I say, be thinking of eating, and drinking, and playing, and buying, and selling, and trading, and the like? Alas! You are yet but a damned man? "Take no thought," says Christ, "what ye shall eat, and what ye shall drink, but seek ye first the kingdom of God" (Matthew 6:33). Let not the condemned prisoner take thought for a supper, but take thought how he may save his neck from the rope. This is the first: if your affections are carnal, so are your thoughts.

Secondly, because if your affections are carnal, so are your lusts. It's true, a godly person has carnal lustings, for they are partly flesh; but then they have good lustings too, for they are partly spirit; the flesh lusts against the spirit, and the spirit against the flesh, and these two are contrary to one another, so that one cannot do as well as one would (Galatians 5:17). They have sinful lustings, but they have spiritual lustings to crucify them; but if your affections are earthly, your lusts are all earthly, indeed, your lusts are ripened and strengthened. The carnal lusts properly and especially are the first offer of the heart unto carnal affections. So that when they come to be carnal affections, they are ripened. And therefore the Apostle usually calls the carnal affections by the name of lusts. "The Gentiles walked in lusts, excess of wine, revellings," etc. (1 Peter 4:3). That is, they walked in their carnal affections; because the lusts are then strengthened when they become affections. Now, beloved, consider what a hideous condition it is to set our affections on the earth, it strengthens our lusts. We give a knife to a cut-throat to stab us, cherish a company of vipers in our bosom to poison us. We encourage fierce enemies to battle against our souls. So Saint Peter can tell us. "Dearly beloved, I beseech you as strangers and pilgrims, abstain from filthy lusts which war against the soul" (1 Peter 2:11). They war against the soul, they are the devil's infantry, yes, chivalry too, they are his soldiers to murder the soul with spiritual death and eternal damnation. If you ever loved your own soul, you would kill sin in the cradle, supplant it and take it by the heel, as Jacob did Esau in the womb, you will never overcome it else. Deny it the first entrance, as the Angel shut the door upon the Sodomites, cast out the bondwoman with her brat too, as Sarah did Hagar and her little one, as Gregory speaks. You will never be able to subdue it otherwise. You would crucify your lusts and mark the first risings thereof, thus you would do, if you had a care of your soul. But will you let your lusts grow, and get armour to kill you? Will you let them gather strength and ripeness to damn you? There is not a lust of them, but it comes like an armed man to fight against your soul; now if you set your affections too on the things of this life, you do strengthen it and weapon it yet more. What a wretched misery is this! Your lusts war against your soul to undo it, and yet you strengthen them; yes, you increase them, help their forces. O fools, when will you understand? Do we not see how we are overpowered by our lusts? Do they not conquer us every day in the open field? There is not a prayer we make, but deadness of heart gets the day like a conqueror. Not a duty we perform, but lukewarmness proves victor. Nay, our lusts do not only overcome us, but they lead us in triumph. Some of our lusts carry us up and down from gaming to fretting, from fretting to revenging, from revenging to swearing, from swearing to lying, from one sin to another, as they please. And our lusts are so strong that war against our souls, that we are not ashamed to lay down our bucklers and say, we cannot resist. "I was angry, alas! It is my nature, and I cannot master it. I let out an oath now and then, alas! I was provoked, and I cannot help it: I must say and do as such an one would have me, he is my friend, I cannot deny him." Thus our lusts have given us mortal wounds and have murdered our souls, and all this is because our affections are earthly, for they increase all our lusts, and make them more able to vanquish us.

Thirdly, if your affections are carnal, so are your purposes: Men purpose according to their affections. He who desires a good bargain will purpose to make it; he who desires pleasure will purpose to seek it; he who desires anything will purpose to obtain it. First, men conceive a thing to be good, then they desire it, and then they think about it, and then they purpose to acquire it if possible. "Barnabas exhorted them all, that with purpose of heart they would cleave unto the Lord" (Acts 11:23). He joins their purpose and their affection to God together: because they could never cleave unto the Lord, but it must be with the purposes of the heart. Now, consider what enemies we are to God, and what enemies we are to our own souls, when we set our affections on earthly things, we can never have genuine purposes to amend or turn to God. We may purpose and purpose a thousand times over, but still, we are broken off from our purposes, they all come to nothing, as long as we desire the things of this life. Can fire have a purpose to freeze? Can a stinking dunghill have a purpose to smell well? Can a swine have a purpose not to wallow in the mire? No, how can this be when they are affected with contrary qualities? There is no counsel in such purposes as these. "Without counsel, purposes are disappointed" (Proverbs 15:22). If you purpose to do this or that, and do not consider whether you are able to do it or not, no wonder you are disappointed in your purpose. You are carnal and have a purpose to be spiritual: you are full of earthly desires and have a purpose to hunger after Christ. You are a company-keeper, worldly, and proud, you have a purpose to be otherwise: Alas! Such purposes as these will surely be disappointed because they lack counsel: you should first seek counsel on how to crucify your affections; if you would do this, your purposes would stand. What an egregious sin it is then, to set your affections on things that are carnal! You are vain and have no purpose to be otherwise; you are secure and have no purpose to shake off security; no purpose to give up your carnal appetites, and your customs, and the lusts that your conscience knows of: your own conscience can point out many lusts that you live in, and you have no purpose to abandon them. O, how does this provoke the Lord Jesus to wrath! Who among us thus purposes in his heart? "I absolutely purpose henceforth to use all the means under Heaven for saving my soul, I have fooled it till this day, now I purpose to do so no more; now I will examine my conscience every day, keep company with the godly every day; I will never associate with my old companions again, I have used my body like an Idol, now I purpose to mortify it," etc. Alas! Our affections will not let us. It is certain, you never have a genuine purpose to God for your soul as long as your affections are earthly. All your purposes are like chaff, says a divine, they last for an hour, or a day, or a season, like the chaff which the wind drives away.

Fourthly, if your affections are carnal, so are your devices and contrivings. When a person sets their affections on anything, as they spend many thoughts on it, and purpose to obtain it if they can, so they devise with themselves ways to achieve it. David's enemies, whose affections were set against him, they devised how they might harm him. "All that hate me, devise my hurt" (Psalm 41:7). What a multitude of devices has the glutton to satisfy their palate? The revengeful person to satisfy their wrath? The covetous person to secure their wealth? It's endless to recount the countless devices people have to attain what their heart desires. Phalaris devises new torments; Nero devises new cruelties; Sardanapalus proposes a reward by a crier to whoever could devise new pleasure. The wicked lawyer and troublesome parishioner devise new legal tricks and scenarios to outwit their neighbour; the proud dandy devises new cosmetics, new grooming habits, new adornments, and the like; the covetous deceiver devises new schemes, new swindles, extortion, deceit, etc. The usurer devises new forms of usury, new agreements and loopholes. It would take long to list all the devices people have to satisfy their unruly affections. These wretches are abhorred by the Lord. Solomon says there are six, yes, seven things, which the Lord hates and abhors (Proverbs 6:16). And in the next verse, he says that a heart that devises wicked imaginations is one of them. The Lord counts these people among the damned crew of the heathen, inventors of evil things (Romans 1:30). "Woe unto them that devise iniquity," says the prophet (Micah 2:1). Now see your woeful condition whoever you are, whose affections are carnal, your devices are all carnal, you do not devise how you may best serve Almighty God, how you may best overcome sin, how you may best glorify Christ. Which of us sets their mind to work every day, how they may best pray, and best repent, and best hear, and best perform every good duty? Alas! There is little such devising among us because our affections do not lean this way.

If our affections were set on God, we would be studying and devising how to purify our families, how to promote the glory of God in the parish, how to encourage, rebuke, and stir up one another to godliness. A generous person devises generous things (Isaiah 32:8), they devise how they may support God's poor saints, how they may employ the poor, how they may further the Gospel with their resources, if possible. A humble person devises humble things, a peaceable person devises peaceable things, a holy person devises holy things: if our affections were right, we would all put our heads together to devise how the parish may best be reformed, how our scandalous practices may best be eliminated, how the Word that we hear from Sabbath to Sabbath may best be put into practice among us; thus it would be if our affections were set on God; but because our affections are not set so, it happens that our devices are carnal.

THE NINTH SERMON

"Set your affections on things that are above, and not on things which are on the earth." – Colossians 3:2

There remains the fourth head, which is the extremity of the affections, and that is zeal. Zeal is due only to God and the things of His worship: and therefore hence we may see how infinitely they sin, that set their affections on things here on earth, because they rob God of His due; zeal, which is the extremity of the affections, is due only to God and the things of His worship. Phinehas was zealous for his God, Num. 25:13, he gave the zeal of his affections to no other but God. Now, what is zeal?

Zeal is a high strain of all the affections, whereby the heart puts forth all its affections with might upon that which it absolutely affects; five things therefore there are, which concur to the making up of zeal.

First, A high measure of the affections. Every measure of the affections is not zeal; a man may affect a thing coldly and lukewarmly, that is not zeal. As a covetous man may have lukewarm good affections to the word. But this is not zeal, I say, zeal is a high measure of the affections. Zeal is a metaphorical word in the Original, it's taken from the seething of water over the fire. Every measure of heat in the water is not seething. No, seething hot is a high measure of heating. The Apostle confesses how the false Apostles affected the Galatians. They zealously affect you, says he, Gal. 4:17. He confesses they did affect the Galatians, and he confesses they did highly affect them, in a very high measure, if it had been as well, as it was high: they zealously affect you, that is, they highly affect you. Clavasius, a Casuist for the Pope, having run through all the Alphabet of questions, in the end of his Book concludes with zeal. Zeal, says he, is a high measure of heat of affection, such an one, says he, as I have shown unto Christ in writing this Book. It's a most devilish saying, for his Book is little else than a hellish rhapsody of blasphemies to Christ, and magnifyings of his holy father the Pope. But therein he says right, that zeal is a high measure of affection.

Secondly, As zeal is a high measure of the affections, so it is of all the affections. I do not say any one of the affections alone, or of sundry together. But it is a high measure of all the affections. Bonaventura and other of the School make it only of love; Ludovicus Vives makes it to be compounded of two affections, indignation and pity. Others to be mixed of anger and love: this is not so: for zeal is a high strain of all the affections. And therefore the Apostle sets it as a general height of the affections in general. "It's good," says he, "to be zealously affected in a good thing," Gal. 4:18. He does not only say, it's good to be zealous in love, or zealously angry, but generally it's good to be zealously affected in a good thing. Sorrow for sin is good, and therefore it's good to be zealously affected with it: Desire of grace is good, and therefore it's good to be zealously affected with it. So that then we may be said to be zealous for God; when our love to him is earnest, our desire of him is earnest, our joy in him is earnest, our indignation against whatever may dishonor him or dislike him, is earnest: when we think nothing too good, nothing too dear, nothing too much to bestow upon him. A man may love God in a lukewarm measure, hate sin in a lukewarm measure, grieve for his corruptions, desire faith and repentance, delight in good duties, pity the miseries of others, fear to transgress God's Commandment, a man may have all these affections thus in a lukewarm measure: as this is displeasing to God, so it is not zeal. Zeal is a high measure, the highest strain of all the affections.

Thirdly, As zeal is the highest measure of all the affections, so it is with all the might of the soul. For when a man does zealously affect anything, his affection is mighty upon it. "Thou shalt love the Lord thy God with all thy heart, and with all thy soul, and with all thy might," Deut. 6:5. That is, thou shalt love him zealously. Nimrod was a mighty hunter, Gen. 10:9. That is, he was zealous at his hunting. "Woe unto them that are mighty to drink wine," Isa. 5:22. That is, that are greedy and zealous in the pursuit of their appetite in that kind. David danced before the Lord with all his might, 2 Sam. 6:14. That is, he did it zealously. Zeal is when the heart raises up its affections with all its might on a thing. And therefore lukewarmness is called negligence in the Scripture: "Cursed is he that doth the work of the Lord negligently." As he that fights negligently, shows not all his might in his fighting, so he that goes about any duty of the Lord's service negligently, his heart does not show all his might in it. It puts not forth all the might of its affections upon it. Lukewarmness then is the negligence of the affection, and cursed is the man that does the work of the Lord negligently, says the Text. But zeal is the might of the affection.

Fourthly, As zeal is with all the might, so it is the putting forth of all the affections. When the heart affects a thing, and puts forth all its affections upon it, reserving no part of its affections for anything else, this

we call zeal. Herod affected the preaching of John, but he did not affect it
zealously, he did not put forth all his affection upon it, he reserved a main
part of his affection for his pleasure. And therefore he was not zealous in
hearing. Hence it is that the Scripture calls lukewarmness deceitfulness,
as Divines do observe; "Cursed is the deceiver," Mal. 1:14. That is, cursed
is the lukewarm person that offers God less than he has; offers somewhat,
and reserves back somewhat, that puts not forth all his affection upon
God and his Service. Zeal is the putting forth of all the affection. As when
the heart affects God, and affects nothing in competition with him, this
is to be zealously affected towards God. When the Jews had crucified
Christ, and persecuted Paul, and forbidden him to preach, the Text says,
the wrath of God was come upon them to the utmost, 1 Thes. 2:16. That
is, the zeal of God's fury, and anger and vengeance was on them. He kept
nothing back; he was not angry a little, nor wroth a little, but he put forth
the affection of his wrath to the utmost upon them. So when the heart
puts forth the utmost of its love upon God, and the utmost of its delights
upon his Word, and the utmost of its fear on his Name, and the utmost
of its affection on his Commandments, then it is zealous; But if he keeps
back ought to bestow it elsewhere, it's a deceiver and a lukewarm heart.

Fifthly, As zeal is the putting forth of all the affection, so it is upon a
thing which the heart does absolutely affect. A man may affect a thing
when he does not affect it absolutely. He affects such or such a thing,
but he does not affect it absolutely. He affects it perhaps with a degree of
affection, as far as twelvepence will go, he places maybe a groat's worth
of affection upon a quire of paper. If he is asked five pounds of silver
for a quire of paper, he does not affect it at that rate, and therefore he
does not affect it absolutely. But if a man has a true zeal of affection for a
thing, he affects that thing with absolute affection, let it cost what it can,
he affects it, let it cost him all charges, and all pains, and all difficulties,

yea, though it cost him his life, he will have it, then he does absolutely affect it. So that then is a man zealous for God and for grace when his affections stand absolutely that way. Maybe he will be glad if he may get it at an easy rate; but if he cannot, alas, he must have it, he concludes upon that, though it cost him sighs, groans, everyday strivings, everyday labor, praying, meditating, repenting, parting with all his lusts, although never so dear. O his soul does affect it in that manner, he must and he will have it, rather than life. This man is zealously affected towards grace, and towards God, because he affects it absolutely. Thus Job was zealous in affecting God's Word, he esteemed it above his necessary food, Job 23:12. He does not say above his daily food, for so he might do, and not be zealously affected therewith; but he affected God's Word above his necessary food, above all food absolutely, without which his life could not consist; without which a man dies: such food as this comes nearest of all outward things to be absolutely affected. A man affects it above lands, and above livings, above his silver and his gold, above all his pleasures and his gamings, a man will part with them all, rather than part with his necessary food. Yet Job affected God's Word above it. And therefore he affected it zealously. This is the last thing in zeal. It is upon that which one does absolutely affect.

Albeit, now it may partly appear by the very definition of zeal, that it is due only to God, a man must not be zealous about anything, nor zealously affected with anything, but only with God and his worship. Nevertheless, we may yet further prove it.

Firstly, Because Zeal is the religious part of the affections of the soul. Now the religious part of them is due only to God.

"I profited in the Jews' Religion, being zealous of the traditions of my Fathers," says Paul, Gal. 1:14. He makes zeal the character of his Religion. Do you see a man zealous then after profits, and most earnest to get means and maintenance and the things of this life? That man makes gain his Religion. Do you see a man zealous after anything? That's his Religion. Zeal is the religious part of the affections, and therefore it's due only unto God.

Secondly, As zeal is the religious part of our affections, so also it is the most of every affection, and therefore only due unto God. Zeal is the most of every act that a man does. That which the mind minds most and studies most, that it minds zealously; that which the memory remembers most, which the heart wills most, it wills zealously. That which a man fears most, and loves most, and desires most, that it does zealously. Now if zeal be the most of every act of the soul, it must needs be idolatry to place it anywhere else but in the service of God. Do you meditate most, and think most of the world? Your thoughts are idolatrous. Do you talk most, and confer most of the things of the world? Your words are idolatrous. Do you care most, and care most? Do you love most, and rejoice most in anything of this life? Your affections are idolatrous. Do you sorrow most for crosses, and losses, and disgraces, and the like, more than you grieve for your sins? Your grief is idolatry. That's the heart's Idol which it does affect most. How often is God in Scripture called the most High? The most High, Act. 7:48. If he is the most high, then the most high of every act and of every affection must be for him. The very Heathen call God, Deus optimus maximus, God the most good, and the most great: so likewise he is the most terrible, and the most holy, and the most just; and therefore the most of our affections must needs be due unto him. Zeal is the most of every one of the affections, and that only is suitable to God. The affections must be suitable to the thing we affect; but nothing of all the affections is suitable to God besides zeal: for zeal is the most of every one of them.

Thirdly, As zeal is the most of every affection, so it is the peculiar pitch of every affection. There cannot be two mosts. The superlative degree cannot be two; Doctissimus properly is a term peculiar to one body: the most learned man in the world is a peculiar word peculiar to one. There may be ten learned, a thousand learned, there may be many learned, but most learned is a peculiar title. So zeal being the most of the affections, it must needs be peculiar to some one thing, which cannot be any other but God. Christ gave himself for us, that he might redeem us from all iniquity, and purchase to himself a peculiar people, zealous of good works, Tit. 2:14. Those people that are zealous of good works, you see they are people peculiar to Christ. They can be no other people but Christ's people that are zealous of good works. No people under heaven are truly zealous of good works, but only his people. This is peculiar to Christ to have such people: because zeal is peculiarly due unto him. You cannot possibly be one of God's people, if you are not zealous for God. A zealous believer, and a zealous repenter, and a zealous professor, zealous in praying, and zealous in hearing the Word. Zealous people are peculiar people to Christ. Under love, and under joy, and under hope, and under fear, are not peculiarly due unto God. For I may love my health too, and I may delight in the blessings of this life, and I may fear a temporary evil. I may lend mine under affections to some things else besides God; but my zeal being the most of my affections, must be given to God, zeal is peculiar to him. You are a worldling then, you are none of God's if you are not zealous for him. You are of your father the devil, you are none of God's unless you are zealous to him. Zeal is his peculiar.

Fourthly, As zeal is the peculiar pitch of every affection, so it is the most spending part of the affections: A man must spend himself upon nothing but God; nothing else will quit charges. Now zeal is the spendingest strain of every affection: It most spendeth the spirits, it most busieth the body: you may gather what a spending thing zeal is, by the passage in the Psalmist. David says thus, "My zeal hath consumed me, because my enemies have forgotten thy words," (Psa. 119:139). David was so zealous for God, that he did even spend himself to see how his enemies dishonoured his God. A child of God is like a faithful servant to his Master, he is willing to spend himself in his service. So he is content to spend himself in his employments for God. Paul when God employed him for the souls of the Corinthians, he says thus, "I will gladly spend and be spent for you," why? What was the reason? "I abundantly love you," says he, (2 Cor. 12:15), that is, he was zealous in his love to their souls, God had employed him for the good of their souls, and he was so zealous in this employment, that he could even spend himself, and be spent for them. And indeed zeal itself is a very spending thing. You are the devil's Martyr that spendest yourself upon the things of this life; you are so wedded thereto, that you spendest your parts and your wits hereabouts, you spendest your thoughts and your time hereupon, you spendest yourself and your spirits this way. The voluptuous man spends himself as much at his sports, as a Minister spends himself in a Pulpit, as a godly man spends himself in good duties. As for God's Service, your prayers are so cold and so negligent, that you spendest yourself not at all in them. Your repentance is so overly, it spends you never a jot to go thorough it: you are so eager after your pleasures, they spend you; so earnest after the world, that spends you, because you are zealous about such things. But it is otherwise with you in the Service of God. This is another strong reason, why zeal is due properly to God, because a man must spend himself upon nothing so much as upon pleasing of God, and doing his will, and seeking his glory. It is true, he may spend himself in his calling. But the greatest part of the spending lieth in this, that he may walk with God in his calling. He spendeth himself in belabouring his heart to work in obedience, to follow his businesses with faith, to go about his earthly employments as before God, to glorify God in all his ways. A man may ground himself upon nothing so much as upon God. Zeal to God makes him a kind of Martyr for Christ.

Fifthly, As zeal is the spending part of all the affections, so likewise zeal is the impatient part of all the affections. It is true, we may desire a good report among men, but our affections must not be impatient; if we cannot have it without bating an inch of a good conscience, our desire must be patient without it. We may grieve for a loss or a trouble, but our affection must not be impatient: if we see God's providence hath sent it, our grief must be patient under it. We may affect these outward blessings of God, but our affections must be patient of a privation, but our affections must be zealous to God; because zealous affections are impatient of the contrary. We must so hate sin against God as to be impatient to endure it: so fear to offend him, as to be impatient of any boldness that way; So love the glory of God as to be impatient of any dishonour to his Name: so zealous to reprove sin in a neighbour, as not to suffer sin in him. "Thou shalt rebuke thy neighbour, and not suffer sin on him," (Lev. 19:17), that is, thou shalt be zealous in rebuking. "A high look and a proud heart I will not suffer," (Psa. 101:5), that is, I will be zealous against it. "I have not suffered my mouth to sin," (Job. 13:30), that is, I have been zealous in the ruling of my tongue. Zeal is the impatient part of all the affections, look what thine affections do zealously affect, they will not suffer the contrary. And therefore the zeal of thine affections must be unto God. Indeed if thine affections be lukewarm to God, you may wish that God might be glorified; but if he be not, you can endure it: You may pray to God for grace to heal you of your deadness; but though he do not, you can bear it. But if thine affections were so far herto, as to be zealous, they would be impatient, you could never endure it. Zeal is the impatient degree of the affections, whereby when the soul does affect a thing, it is impatient without it. And therefore zeal is due only to God. Thus you discern the evidence of this truth, that the zeal of our affection is due properly to God.

The Tenth Sermon

"Set your affections on things that are above, and not on things which are on the earth." – Colossians 3:2

The Uses of this are these.

First, Hence we may learn that God demandeth the zeal of our affections: If the zeal of our affections be due unto God, I beseech you take notice that God demandeth his due. "Give unto the Lord the glory due unto his Name," and so God demandeth his due in our affections. "If I be a Father, where is my honour? If a Master, where is my fear?" (Malachi 1:6). He does not only call for some honour, and some love, and some fear, but he calls for his part, "Where is my part?" says he. "Where is my fear?" God's part of thy fear, as I have shown, is the zeal of thy fear, God's part of thy love, and thy joy, and thy hope, and the rest, is the zeal of the same. This now God demands of thy soul; "Where is my fear?" maybe thou lovest him a little, and his Commandments a little, maybe thou fearest him a little, to offend him and disobey him thou fearest a little; this is not God's part, the zeal of thine affection is God's part, and he calls for his part, "Where is my fear?"

Secondly, Hence we may learn that we must, upon pain of God's infinite displeasure, give him the zeal of our affections: whensoever we pray, to pray to him zealously, bleeding for our sins, and melting under our wants, and yearning for his graces. Whensoever we praise him, to praise him thus zealously, rejoicing in his mercies, and admiring his goodness. Whensoever we enter his Courts, to enter with zeal, reverencing his footstool, trembling at his Word; in all our ways seeking how we may be most zealous of his glory: for if God demand the zeal of our affections, there is no keeping back. Ananias was smitten dead for keeping back a little piece of money, when God did demand it. "Cursed is he that keeps back a blow, when God doth call for it": God demandeth our zeal, and woe is us if we keep back.

Thirdly, Hence we may gather that we are in the state of damnation if we do not give God the zeal of our affections: if God require it upon pain of damnation, and we are bid to give it him upon pain of his everlasting displeasure, then certainly we must needs be in a state of damnation if we do not give it. Now this is proved by four Arguments.

First, That man is in the state of damnation who never repents. I need not prove that; you know it well enough. He is sure to perish who never repents. Though you have taken up all the outward duties of religion, you never repent unless you are zealous; if you are zealous, then you have drawn out of Christ's wine-seller, as Bernard observes on the Canticles, "Introduxit me rex in cellam vinariam," the King has brought me into his wine-seller, he expounds it of the soul's drawing of zeal from Christ; but if you are not zealous in repentance, you never repent. "Be zealous and repent," (Revelation 3:19). First, he says, be zealous, and then he says repent. First, you must resolve to be zealous, or else you do not repent: If a man has wronged a neighbour though never so mean, he must be sorry for it, or else he does not repent of it: if a man has wronged a Nobleman, he must be more sorry: for as the wrong is greater, the greater the party wronged is, so the greater is the sorrow that is required to repentance. If a man has wronged the King, it must be a greater sorrow yet, till the sorrow is somewhat answerable to the greatness of the King who is wronged. But if a man has wronged a God, this must be the greatest sorrow of all sorrows, otherwise you do not repent. Repentance is the rending or breaking of the heart, so says the Prophet Joel, it is not lukewarm, or a little grief that will break the heart. Repentance is the humbling of the soul, says David, it is not a little bowing and a little bending will humble it before God. Repentance is the mortifying or the killing of sin, as Paul calls it: alas! Sin is like the heart of an oak that will be a hundred years dying, so sin will be long dying, it is not a little pricking and a little compunction that will kill it. Repentance is called repentance unto life, in the Scripture; it is not a little chafing, and a little rubbing, and a little Aqua-vitae that will fetch a man from death unto life: No, no, beloved: you never repent unless you are zealous. And therefore the Apostle makes zeal a part of repentance, (2 Corinthians 7:11). No zeal, no repentance: no repentance, no salvation.

2.   That man is in the state of damnation who is not a believer in Christ: If a man is not in Christ by a lively faith, he cannot be saved. The Prophet prophesying of Christ, says thus: "Unto us a child is born, and he shall be called wonderful, the Prince of peace: and the zeal of the Lord of hosts shall perform this," (Isaiah 9:6-7). Never is Christ conceived in any man under heaven, but the zeal of the Lord of Hosts does perform it: Does he enlighten the mind, or purge the heart, or cleanse the conscience? Zeal does perform it. Can I be so in love with Christ, as to deny myself for him, and not be zealous for him? Can I count all my parts, and all my gifts, and all that I have, as Paul did, to be dross and dung for the worth I find in Christ, and not be zealous of

him? Can I hunger after him, and pant for him, and be sick of love till I have him, and not be zealous towards him? Thus we must do, otherwise we are not in Christ. And therefore Moses confounds faith and zeal, as if they were all one, and both in one. Phinehas was zealous for God's sake, (Numbers 25:11). That is, he was zealous and faithful both, for so the Psalmist expounds it, "that was counted to him for righteousness," says he, speaking of his zeal in executing of judgment, "that was counted to him for righteousness." Now you know nothing can be counted to a man for righteousness, but only faith, and therefore by zeal there is meant faith. This is an undeniable argument, If a man has faith, he is zealous, otherwise he has no faith. If he has no faith, he cannot be saved.

3.   That man is in the state of damnation who loves not God. "He that loves not the Lord Jesus Christ, let him be Anathema Maranatha," that is, let him be accursed and accursed, for it is the greatest curse in the world, it is the curse of the Gospel, "Let him be accursed, and double accursed, that loves not Christ." Now a man never loves God if he is not zealous: "qui non zelat, non amat": He that is not zealous in love does not love, love is termed zeal in the Scripture. Jehu, indeed the truth was, he had no love to God, he thought he had though; and therefore when he would tell Jehonadab he had love to God, he tells it in these words, "Come and see my zeal I have to the Lord of Hosts," (2 Kings 10:16). That is, see the love that I bear to the Lord of Hosts, "Zelus debet esse non modo in affectu, verum etiam in intellectu," is a saying: zeal must be in the mind, and zeal must be in the affections, both are required to this zeal that I speak of. If you are not zealous, it is most certain, you have not a jot of true love. Zeal is more seen in that affection than any, if there be any; and therefore if there is no zeal in you to God and his ways, there is no love, you are yet under wrath.

4.   That man is in the state of damnation who was never taught of God: Christ promises that all who are His shall be taught of God; taught to be holy as He is holy, to love one another, to walk in all newness of life. Every person is zealous for what they are taught. Paul, before his conversion, was zealous for the ceremonies and traditions of his fathers. "I was taught," says he, "according to the perfect manner of the Law of the Fathers, and was zealous" (Acts 22:3). Alas! If he had been better taught, he would have been better zealous. I do not speak only of outward teaching but also of inward teaching of the heart; his very heart, under the policy of Satan, was taught these things, and therefore he was zealous for them. The covetous man's heart is taught to be earthly, so he is zealous for the world. The proud man's heart is taught to be proud, so he is zealous for his credit and esteem. The voluptuous man's heart is taught to be vain, so he is zealous for his pleasures. Alas! These were never taught of God. The devil and their lusts teach them, and the examples of others teach them. If you are not taught of God how to walk in newness of life, you cannot be saved; it is better to be unborn than untaught, and this, as you see, cannot happen without zeal for God.

5.   That man is in the state of damnation who cannot be pitied. If you are zealous for the things of this life and not for heaven, zealous for your pleasure and not for God's glory, you are not to be pitied. If you desire pleasures, take them, and if you wish to go to hell, go—who will pity you? "Deformitas sceleris aufert misericordiam" (The deformity of wickedness removes pity). It is true, it would cause pity to see a soul weeping and howling for sins yet going to hell. It would pity to see a blind Papist fervently performing religious acts in his blindness, all to save his soul, yet going to hell. It would cause pity to see such a man go to hell, but how can it be otherwise? Yet, it would pity to see him, as he is zealous for God in the blindness of his zeal. As it pitied the

Apostle to see his brethren, who were zealously devoted to God but lacked knowledge, perish. But who will pity you to see you go to hell? You have no zeal towards God at all, you are zealous for the things of this life and your lusts. As God told Jerusalem, "Who shall have pity upon thee, O Jerusalem? Thou hast forsaken me" (Jeremiah 15:5). Who will pity our drunkards and our whoremongers? Who will pity those who are zealous in their sins and abominations? You are not even the objects of pity.

Is it true that the zeal of our affections is due only to God? Is it true that God demands it? And that we are bound upon pain of death and damnation to give it to God? Is it true that if we never repented, never believed, never were in Christ, never loved God, never were taught of God, never can be pitied unless we give the zeal of our affections to God? Then, let us consider the lamentable condition we are in as long as the zeal of our affection runs otherwise. I beseech you to consider these eight things which may convince you of the woeful condition you are in.

Firstly, zeal is the fire of the soul. Whatever you are most zealous about sets your soul on fire. Every man and woman in the world is set on fire by either hell or heaven. If heaven has not ignited you, then hell has. You are ignited by one of these two. As it is the most blessed thing to be ignited by heaven, to be zealous for the glory of God, and the salvation of one's soul; zealous for obtaining grace, and zealous in the duties of religion; so, on the contrary, it is the most cursed thing to be ignited by hell. If you are a swearer, a liar, a filthy speaker, whose mouth speaks vanity, your tongue is set on fire by hell; "the tongue is set on fire of hell," says the Apostle (James 3:6). If you are a voluptuous person who loves pleasures and delights in vanity more than in better things, your heart is set on fire by hell. If you yield to the temptations of Satan—if the devil tempts you to go proudly in your apparel, and you yield; if the devil tempts you to smother your conscience, and you consent; if the devil tempts you to delay your obedience, and the temptation takes hold—every temptation of Satan is a fiery dart, "the fiery darts of the devil" (Ephesians 6:16). The Apostle rightly calls them fiery darts of the devil, as Saint Chrysostom says, for such are the sinful lusts and affections; they are all fiery, set on fire by hell. This is one misery, and it is not a small one; zeal is the fire of the soul, and if it is not set upon God, it is set on fire by hell.

Secondly, zeal is the running of the soul. If you are not zealous for God, you are running after the things of this world; you are not merely going after vanities, but you are running. You are not only pursuing your pleasures and profits, but you are running. As the affections are the feet of the soul, zeal is the swift running pace of these feet. "I will run the way of thy Commandments," says David, meaning he will be zealous in it. The journey to heaven is long, especially now since the fall; it is a very long journey to heaven, and death will overtake us before we can get there unless we run. Therefore, Saint Paul commands us to run fast enough, lest we never get there. "So run that ye may obtain," (1 Corinthians 9:24). Don't we need to set our zeal right? For the way we run reflects where our zeal stands. If the zeal of our affection is directed towards God, we run onwards to heaven; but if it is directed towards earthly things, we run onwards to hell. We hear of Tiberius Nero, who, when his brother Drusus lay sick in Germany, ran two hundred miles in twenty-four hours to visit him. But we may find even faster runners in sin: some in drunkenness and camaraderie, as they call it; others in security and hardness of heart; others in one sin, and others in another. As they run themselves, they wonder why those stricter than themselves do not run with them into the same excess of riot (1 Peter 4:4). Perhaps sometimes they have sudden and intense affections for good, as if they were all on fire momentarily, like the young man in the Gospel who came running to Christ and knelt down before him (Mark 10:17). Oh, he was in a hurry; he didn't walk to Christ, he ran. Many men and women experience very good moods and intense pangs of goodness now and then, but alas! It was nothing but a fleeting moment. Soon after, they were as ready to leave as they were eager to come. Then they continue running in their security and covetousness of mind. Do you not see how fast many of you run in arrears with God? If we could see God's debt-book, might we not read there: "Item, ten thousand oaths you have sworn. Item, millions of filthy words you have spoken. Item, a hundred million wicked thoughts you have thought. Item, a thousand lazy prayers you have made. Item, twenty hundred Sabbaths you have profaned. Item, forty Sacraments you have unworthily received"? This is how you have been running, as if you thought every day was seven years until you reach hell. This is your condition when your zeal is set anywhere else but on God.

Thirdly, zeal is the predominant element in the soul. Whatever the soul is zealous for, that is the predominant temper of the soul: if you are zealous for God, Christ is predominant in you; if you are zealous for the things of this world, the world is predominant in you. "There is no temper but something is predominant," says the Philosopher. You have never heard of a soul that had as much of the world in it as of Christ, or of Christ as of the world. No, as one is zealous for one thing, so one thing or another is predominant in them. Pleasing men is predominant in one, pride predominant in another, and pleasure predominant in a third. Whatever a person is zealous for, that is their predominant element. Now, if your affections, if their zeal, are not set upon God, then something else in the world is predominant in you. Oh, what a misery it is to be less zealous for God than for the world! The world is predominant in you; this is the characteristic of someone who is no better than a reprobate. "Lovers of pleasure more than lovers of God," (2 Timothy 3:4), when pleasure is predominant and not God. "He that loveth father or mother more than me is not worthy of me," says Christ (Matthew 10:37), when carnal relations are predominant, and not spiritual. This is a clear characteristic of a wicked person: for what difference is there between a godly person and a wicked person? Both have sin in them; this is the difference: a godly person has sin in them, but grace is predominant, and therefore they are called godly. A wicked person has many good graces in them, but sin and wickedness are predominant, and therefore they are called wicked. The denomination is from the part that is predominant. The beasts of the earth are named after the earth because the earth is predominant; the fish of the sea are named after the water because the water is predominant; a brick house is so named not because there is no wood in it, but because brick is predominant. Take note of all your thoughts: which is predominant in you, the world or Christ? Observe all your speeches: which is predominant, earthly matters or heavenly ones? Consider all your concerns: which predominates and keeps you busiest? Oh, what a woeful state you are in when sin and corruption are predominant in you! If you are more zealous for the things of this life than for grace and holiness, without which no one shall see the Lord, you can never enter into God's kingdom because sin is predominant in you.

Fourthly, zeal is the self-cruelty of the soul. If you are most zealous for God, your zeal is a holy cruelty to yourself. "Master, spare thyself," says Peter to Christ, "Get thee behind me, Satan," says Christ; he was zealous for the redemption of the world, and he would not spare his own life. Zeal is a holy cruelty of the soul; it will spare nothing, neither life, nor credit, nor living, nor anything. M. Fox, who was zealous in his love for the poor, was in a holy manner cruel to himself, willing to give the very clothes off his back rather than the naked should not be covered. "Love is as strong as death, and as cruel as the grave," (Song of Solomon 8:6). *Durus sicut inferi zelus*, as Ambrose expounds it: zeal is as hard as the grave. A person who is zealous is hard on themselves; they are merciful to their own soul under heaven, not that true zeal is hard and cruel to their own soul, but I mean, to their own fleshly desires and respects, they are the most merciful to their own soul. Now, see what a woeful state you are in if you are not zealous for God: for if the zeal of your affections is directed elsewhere, you are the cruelest person to your own soul indeed and in truth. You squander God's mercies, you treasure up God's wrath, you live in those sins which your own conscience can tell you are sins, you bestow your affections upon the things of this life which should be given to God, you damn your own soul. The time that God gives you to acquire grace, you waste on vanity; you are more concerned for the well-being of your body than for the everlasting welfare of your soul; you part with Christ rather than with your lusts. Oh, you are *durus ut inferi*, as cruel as hell to your own soul. You know that whoever comes to the Sacrament unworthily, or unpreparedly, or not as a new creature, eats and drinks their own damnation; you know this well enough, the Lord says so in his Word. Yet you are so cruel to your own soul that you will venture nonetheless; you know that those who come to this supper without a wedding garment shall be cast into utter darkness, where there is weeping and gnashing of teeth; you know this full well, and you cannot deny it. Yet you are so cruel to your own soul as to come here without it: your affections are so eager for the things of this life, the very zeal of them all, that you are even cruel to your own soul, *Durus ut inferi*, as cruel as hell itself to yourself. Oh, the cruelty of your earthly zeal; it makes you fearless and witless to sin against God, which the Angels of heaven would not do for a thousand worlds. It makes you sin against Christ and cast off his yoke, without which you can never be saved; it makes you suppress the motions of God's Spirit and strangle your own conscience, Durus ut inferi zelus, we may well say; this zeal is as cruel as hell, and yet it is in everyone of us who are not zealous for God.

Fifthly, zeal is the brand of the soul. When a person is zealous in any passion, whatever it may be, it sets a brand upon them; we call them a choleric person, who is zealous with anger; we say they are very touchy. We call them a fretful, envious person who is zealously inclined towards that. We call them a melancholy person who is often in sadness. Zeal, which is the much of every affection, sets a brand upon a person. So when a person is zealous for good, it sets a good brand upon them, as Aemilius was called Aemilius the good for his goodness. Antoninus was called Antoninus the pious for his piety; in Scripture, one Barsabas was called Justus the just. It appears too that Simon was noted for some passionate and affectionate forwardness, and therefore he was called Simon the Zealot (Luke 6:15). Thus, we see that though it may be considered mockery by the ignorant world, it is observed by those outside that God's people are zealous. Look at whatever a person is zealous in; that is able to brand them. Now, if you are zealous for the world or zealous for your pleasures or anything else in the world, it brands you on the forehead as a carnal wretch: like Elymas the sorcerer or Judas the traitor, it stigmatizes you as a worldling, a drunkard, a company-keeper, voluptuous, or whatever it is that you are most zealous for. Every person is more zealous for one thing than for another, either for God or something else in the world; the question is, for what are you most zealous? If you are more zealous for anything else than you are for God, it brands you as a wretch, such a one as a worldling, a miser, a spendthrift, a gambler, or a reveller; it brands you as a hard person. Where your greatest zeal lies, that truly brands you before God and good men who are able to discern you.

THE ELEVENTH SERMON.

"Set your affections on things that are above, and not on things which are on the earth." – Colossians 3:2

The sixth point is, Zeal is the transportation of the soul out of itself. When a person is zealous in a passion, they are transported out of themselves; the passion has command of them, and not they of their passion. Like a person who is consumed with anger or fury, it transports them, and they are under the sway of their anger; their anger rules them. If their anger is righteous, then it is well for them; but if it is carnal, what a woeful condition they are in! If a person's zeal is good and for God, they are blessed. Like David, who was zealous for God, he was transported out of himself; he was not his own master. "No," says he, "I am yours, Lord, save me, for I have sought your precepts" (Psalm 119:94). He pursued God's precepts with such zeal that he was not his own master; he was captivated by his zeal for God, saying, "I am yours." He was at God's disposal, not his own, for his zeal transported him out of himself. He would have transgressed by himself, but his zeal would not allow it. He might have been careless, but his zeal would not permit it. He had to act as his zeal dictated. He did not have command over himself. No, he was at the command of his gracious zeal. It was fortunate for him that it was good. Conversely, if a person's affections are set on the things of this life, they must pursue pleasures, livelihood, and sustenance; they are zealous for them. Such a person is not their own master; they are slaves to their desires. As David said, "I am yours, Lord," so they may say, "I am yours, World; I am yours, Pleasure; I am yours, Satan; I am at your command and in your service." As the text says, Paul, a servant of Jesus Christ; Jude, a servant of Jesus Christ, for they were zealous for Christ, and their zeal made them not their own masters. Similarly, I may say of a wicked person, Esau, a servant of sinful pleasure and delights; Demas, a servant of this present world; Diotrephes, a servant of his own ambition; for they were zealous for these things, and their zeal made them slaves to them. "Everyone who commits sin is a slave to sin," says Christ to the Jews (John 8:34). "Slave?" they say, "We were never slaves; we are free." "Slaves," he says, "Yes, you are slaves to sin, for you seek to kill me." Are you not slaves to sin when you obediently follow your desires, even to the point of committing murder? I know there are two kinds of slaves and servants: some are in close custody, such as those who are kept so confined that they cannot venture beyond profanity. Others are in false custody. When a person's desires hold them on a longer leash, like birds in a larger cage, they may be free to be religious, attend church, hear the word, pray, and be civil. But when they reach the end of their leash, their desires pull them back. The former are slaves to their base desires, chained to their seats and oars; the latter are their sluggish messengers, sent on errands. Therefore, the devil, who takes advantage of a person's desires, is said to hold them captive at his will (2 Timothy 2:26). You may say, "I am not the devil's captive at his will; I will not swear, swagger, or be drunken as some do." Alas, alas! It is not the devil's pleasure for you to be a drunkard or a swearer; he uses his servants for different purposes. It is not his pleasure for you to employ your tongue in swearing; no, he will use your tongue only to talk civilly about worldly matters. It is not his pleasure to lead you into drunkenness and whoredom, but to lead you into a life of security, formality, and presumption. Oh, what a dreadful state you are in when the zeal of your affections is not set upon God! What will your affections not command? And when they command, you are not your own master; you must obey. Let covetousness command; how will you shorten your prayers in the morning? How seldom will you think of God throughout the day? How will you worry, pinch, and save? Let merriment and revelry command you; how will you joke, fool around, play, and mock, all for amusement? Let revenge command you; how angrily will you look? How snappishly will you speak? How rudely will you clench your fist? Or how basely will you scheme to cause harm? How quick will you be to misinterpret your neighbour's actions? How ready to entertain any malicious gossip about them? Thus, you are not your own master but harassed and driven by your unruly affections until they have ruined your soul forever. Oh, consider the wretchedness of your slavery when the zeal of your affections is thus separated from God. Consider quickly, for if your affections keep you in service for long, they will keep you forever. The longer a person remains in service, the more foolish they are. Alterius ne sit, qui suus esse potest: In the Law of God, it is written that if a servant still loves his master after seven years of bondage, the Law says this: let his master bore his ears, and make him serve forever (Exodus 21:5). Therefore, beware; if you love to live as you do, and you like your slavish ways too much, beware, I say, lest your ears be nailed to your affections, and you be made a slave forever. I fear we have many such slaves, with their ears pierced and their souls apprentices to the ways of Death.

Seventhly, Zeal is the strength of the soul; zeal carries all the strength of the soul with it, leaving none behind. And therefore, the Scripture puts these two things together: one's zeal and his strength. "Lord, where is thy zeal and thy strength?" says the Prophet, Isa. 63:15. If he asks where his zeal is, he asks where his strength is, for zeal is the strength of the soul. You know Jacob wrestled with God for a blessing, and his effectual fervent prayer prevailed, but how does God express it? He expresses his zeal thus. "By his strength he had power with God," Hos. 12:3. His prayer was a zealous prayer, and therefore it was a prayer with strength. By his strength he had power with God. He prayed, and he prayed with strength; he laid all his strength that he could on the duty, and by his strength he had power with God. Look what a man is zealous unto, all his strength goes to it; he leaves none behind.

Oh, the misery of a carnal heart that is not zealous for God; he has no strength at all left for God or the saving of his soul. Would he pray? Alas! He has no strength to pray with. His prayers are as weak as bulrushes. Would he resist sin? He has no strength to resist it with. His striving to resist it is nothing able. Oh, how hardy he is to commit sin! The charges and the cost that are in drinking do not terrify the drunkard from his drunkenness; the cost that is in garish apparel does not terrify the proud from their vanity in clothes. The disgrace that is in sin does not terrify the adulterer from his lust. The fear of fathers and mothers' displeasure does not terrify the spendthrift from his riot. No, wicked men are hardy that way because their zeal goes that way. But to that which is good, how weak is thy heart? Ezek. 16:30. Nihil metuendum vidit, metuit tamen: the least cross look of a father or a mother or a great man scares him. One twelve-penny charge affrights him. One petty difficulty dampens him because his zeal stands towards another point.

Take him at the plough; there he can be strong to labour; he will toil, he will sweat, he will hold out. Take him at prayer; he is as weak as water. Take him at a tale or a story; he will remember it well and repeat it after you; his memory is strong. Take him at a sermon; his memory fails him. Take him in a business to manage; his wit is strong, his parts strong, he has an excellent reach. But take him in mortification; he is as weak as a man without understanding. This is the misery of thy soul when thy zeal is not set upon God.

The devil is the strong man, Mat. 12:29. and thou hast no strength to encounter him. Thy lusts are strong to enthrall thee, and thou hast no strength to be free, and yet thou pissest at these things. Men think nothing of the devil, as though he were nothing but a scarecrow. They defy him every hour in the day; they jest at him, saying the devil is a fool. They'll paint him on their walls and call for him as though they would give him a challenge. I remember a pretty proverb that I read the Germans have: "Non pingendus est Diabolus in pariete, quia sponte sua venit." Paint not the devil on the wall; he will come soon enough of his own accord. I am sure he comes too soon to beguile men, too soon to bewitch and befool men, too soon to disarm men from all strength to that which is good. If he can once set thine affections on the things of this life, he has gotten the victory, and thou art not able to recover.

Eighthly, Zeal is the full confidence of the soul: that which a man chiefly trusts in is what he is most zealous about. He who is zealous for the world trusts in the world, otherwise he would not be zealous for it. He trusts to have pleasures, goods, and esteem if he is zealous about them. What, do you trust to bear all before you? As we say when we see a man hot and zealous about anything, the soul would not be zealous but that it truly trusts to prevail. "Thus shall mine anger be accomplished, and they shall know that I the Lord have spoken it in my zeal," Ezek.

5:13. God was confident of the fulfilling of his wrath; why? Because he had spoken in his zeal. Indeed, God may well be so, were he never so little angry, but the words do express the nature of zeal. It's the full trust of the soul to succeed.

A wise man will not be hot upon anything unless he trusts to go through with it. If zeal then be the full trust of the soul, what a mad man art thou not to be zealous for God? Thou trustest in the world, thy pleasures, and thy passions; thou dost not trust God. If thou trusted the Lord God, thou wouldst be zealous for God. Alas, alas! Thou canst not trust God; thou never labours to please him. He that depends on a man and must trust him for help and assistance will not offend him. Alas! What trust can he have in him if he offends him continually? When the Sydonians and the Tyrians had offended King Herod, their country being nourished by the King's country, Acts 12:20, they laboured to please him again. So if thou wouldst trust Almighty God, thou wouldst labour to please him and to be zealous for his name, and not make him thine enemy by thy sins and iniquities. Thou who blasphemes his name with thine oaths, abuses his creatures with thy intemperance, and profanes his ordinances with thy carelessness and neglect, and displeases him all the year long. Alas! How canst thou trust him? Thou makest him thine enemy; canst thou trust one who vows to hang thee? Thou art a damned man if God does not pardon thee. Thou art a woeful wretch, better thou hadst never been born if God does not give thee grace. And canst thou trust God he will be good to thee when thou displease him day by day, offend him every step? No, no, thou mayst trust him; he will confound thee. Thou who art a liar, thou mayst trust him; what he says in the Apocalypse, "All liars shall be cast into the lake of brimstone." Thou who art a swearer, mayst trust him; he will never hold thee guiltless. Thou who art a drunkard, a company-keeper, and a whoremonger, mayst trust him; thou shalt never inherit the kingdom of heaven. Thou who talkest idly and unprofitably, mayst trust him; he will call thee to account at the day of judgment. Thou who hardenest thy neck against the reproofs of the word, mayst trust him; he will destroy them without remedy. This he has promised, and herein thou mayst trust him: thou canst never trust him for mercy or grace or any good thing; thou displeasest him daily and makest him thine enemy. And how canst thou trust him? What thinkest thou? Does he not know how little thou carest for his commandments? How little thou respectest his ordinances? How basely thou usest him in thy ways? Indeed, if thou wert zealous for his glory and zealous to please him in holiness of life, obedient and seeking him, then thou mightest trust him. Thou canst never trust him otherwise. By this time, thou mayst see what a woeful condition thou art in if the zeal of thine affections be not set upon God.

But many poor souls may demand, how then shall I know whether the zeal of mine affections be set upon God? I answer thee: There are seven signs whereby thou mayst know it.

The first, If thine affections be notable to Godward: a man may have a little hope, and a little grief, and a little joy, and a little pity, and nobody see it. But if it be zealous, it will quickly be notable; everyone, when once it is zealous, everyone will note it. When Epaphras was zealous to save souls in Colossae, what says Saint Paul of him? I bear him record, he hath a great zeal for you, says he, Colossians 4:13. Paul could not but note it in him; he saw so many strong expressions of it.

This holiness and forwardness is very remarkable. But if on the contrary there be no notable expressions of grace in you, alas! There may be some goodness, some pity, some grief, some motions; but this is no zeal, it is not remarkable. If a man be zealous for the world, his scraping and sparing are notable, his toiling and studying, and talking that way is very notable. I will bear him record, he is a worldling; the world is so much in his speeches, the world is so much in his courses, and so much in his face. Look upon his ways, he is so encumbered with thoughts of the world: Look into his family, there be so few good duties of grace, and so many tokens of the world: Look upon his meetings, his discourses of edifying are so scarce, and of the world are so copious, I will bear him in record, he is a worldling. Were we zealous for God, there would be diverse signs and expressions of our zeal unto God. Saint Paul when he would make it plain to the Corinthians, that he was an Apostle to them, he tells them, truly the signs of an Apostle were wrought among you, 2 Corinthians 12:12. If we were zealous for God, ye might answer, Truly the signs of true zealots are wrought among us: ye that profess Christ, what signs of true zealots are there in you? If your brethren be secure and grown-dull, do ye labour to quicken them? If the Gospel do not thrive, do ye labour to further it? If grace be little stirring in the Parish, does Heaven ring with your groans and your prayers? If zeal were existent among you, it would be notable and remarkable among you, we might say, I bear you record it is so, nay, the wicked without would observe it, we bear them record, they keep a great stir about heaven, our lives would convince them. Maybe they would hate us and reproach us the more: but this is certain, our lives would convince them, as Christ's did the Centurion, doubtless this is a righteous man, Luke 23:47. So your lives would convince all their consciences; doubtless they are strict men, doubtless they are humble, and meek, and religious. Thus it would be, were we zealous. But if our religion be not notable, hardly notable to ourselves, we can hardly tell whether we have true faith and repentance, and zeal at all, yea or no: much less notable to others, it is to be feared ye are not zealous for God.

The second sign of zeal towards God is, to be impatient of sin. Zeal, as aforesaid, is the impatient part of the affections: if a man do affect a thing but a little, he can be patient without it; but if he affect it very deep and with zeal, O his affections are set on it, and he is impatient if he speed not. So that if thou beest zealous against sin, thou art impatient of sin, thou canst not suffer it. Zeal is impatient of whatever is contrary to it. That this is the nature of zeal, you may see by the poor blind zeal that was in Paul before his conversion: he was zealous to God as he thought, and thinking that the Church of Christ were contrary to all men, enemies to God and man, therefore now in the blindness of his zeal he persecutes that way unto death: Concerning zeal I persecuted the Church, Philippians 3:6. It was a woeful kind of zeal to persecute the Church, but yet there you may gather the nature of zeal, it cannot abide that which is contrary: and therefore if thou beest zealous against sin, thou canst not abide sin; better journey, riding, studies, prayers, exhortations, any course thou wilt use, rather than abide it: thou canst never abide anything that is displeasing to God, but resist it to the utmost, and this resisting will be,

First Universal: If thou beest zealous, there is no sin thou canst possibly abide. Nothing is cold but the fire does resist it; so nothing is sin but zeal does resist it to the utmost. I esteem all thy precepts concerning all things to be right; I hate every false way, Psalm 119:128. This is zeal indeed, there is never a false way that a man can abide that is zealous. To be zealous against one sin, and lukewarm against another, this is not zeal.

Secondly, General, in all manner of persons.

First, In a friend as well as in an enemy: If thou beest zealous, thou wilt find fault with thy friends when they sin, as well as observe a fault when thine enemy offendeth. Men are apt to observe when their enemy sinneth, O how unconscionable is he! Thus he hath done, and so he hath done; but if thou beest zealous, when thy friend does transgress, thou wilt not abide it. Fire will not only labour to consume the water that comes to put it out, but also the wood that comes to maintain it. So it is with zeal, Do not I hate them that hate thee? Says David to God, Psalm 139:21. He could not abide to count them his friends that were not friends unto God, though otherwise they were very friends unto him, and may be saved his life, and were patrons and benefactors unto him, he could not wink at their sins, because they were his friends: though thy friend be a swearer or a carnal wretch, yet if he be thy friend, and thou dependest upon him, thou canst see it and not see it; but if thou beest zealous, all his sins thou wilt count discourtesies to thee.

Secondly, In one's child as well as a servant, you shall have many, they are angry at every sin a servant commits; but if their children do sin, they connive; it was no such great fault, alas! He did it unwittingly, and what would ye have a child do? Say they: they can excuse it in their children, and lessen it; but if thou beest zealous, thou canst not abide sin in thy son anymore then a servant, thou wilt correct him, and curb him, and threaten him, and counsel him, and never endure he should sin, if thou canst possibly help it. What, my son, and be wicked? What do I love God, and shall I suffer my loins to dishonour him? Son, know thou the God of thy father, otherwise I count thee a bastard, and no son. This brake old Eli's neck, because he suffered his sons to be wicked, when he by godly severity might have remedied it. A zealous man when his son hath committed things worthy of death, will not spare him, Zechariah 13:3.

Thirdly, In one's own wife or husband, or father or mother, as well as in a neighbour, zeal cannot abide it; husband thou dost not love me as long as thou livest thus; wife, thy heart is not with me as long as thou dost thus; how canst thou love me when thou dost not love God nor thine own soul? This is the meaning of our Saviour: If any come to me, and hate not father and mother, and wife, and children, and brethren, and sisters, yea, and his own life, he cannot be my Disciple. Luke 14:26. A zealous man cannot abide to yield to sin, for the best of them all.

Fourthly, In a rich man as well as in a poor man, if thou beest zealous, thou canst not abide sin, neither in the rich, nor in the poor: if poor men offend, and if beggars be idle and ungodly, then thou wilt complain; Oh, the poor are so wicked, they break down our hedges, who would relieve them? They will not be orderly, they lie drinking in Ale-houses, and spend it away on the pot, therefore who would relieve them? But if the rich be keepers of company, and vain in their pleasures, thou art not so zealous against their sins, alas! This is no zeal: but let a wicked man be as great as King Ahab, Micaiah will deal roundly with him. Nehemiah will not spare Lord's nor Nobles when they sin, Nehemiah 13:17. For a Magistrate to punish poor Malefactors, and not the Gentry, when they do transgress, is this zeal? No it is cursed partiality.

Fifthly, In one's self, rather than in anybody else; true zeal is more zealous against sin in one's self than in all the world besides; otherwise, says our Saviour, it is hypocrisy and not zeal. Thou hypocrite, first cast out the beam out of thine own eye, and thou shalt see clearly to cast out the mote out of thy brother's eye, Matthew 5:7. Zeal I say, is like unto fire, it is hot itself first, before it heat others: may be the fire meets with many other things that it is not able to heat it, as the bottom of a kettle of water, the fire cannot heat it, nevertheless the fire will be sure to be hot of itself. So it is with thee: if thou beest zealous against sin, thou wilt be like unto fire, rather suffer cold to be in any other, then suffer it to be in itself; so thou wilt rather suffer sin in anybody else, then suffer it in thyself: thou wilt not suffer sin anywhere else by thy good will, but above all things thou wilt not suffer it in thyself. This is the second sign of zeal towards God, it is impatient of sin.

The third sign of zeal towards God is that it cannot be quiet until it is assured of God's favour and of Christ. You are never earnest for God if you can be at peace without assurance of Christ and of Heaven. The reason is plain, I need not express it. I know many a child of God is not assured hereof, but there is never a child of God under heaven who is not restless until he is. Alas! He is never zealous for God if he is content without assurance of God's love in Christ Jesus. Can I zealously love him, whose love to me I am not assured of? For all that I know, he will cut my throat, he will turn into the sorest enemy I have. I cannot zealously love him. No more can you zealously love God as long as you are content without the assurance of his love. For all that you know, God does not love you, God may damn you and cast you to hell forever, and turn into the sorest enemy in the world to your soul, for all that you know, and therefore you cannot zealously love him. If then you are a zealous lover of God, either you are assured of his love, or you can never be content without it. "Give diligence," says the Apostle, "to make your calling and election sure, for if you do these things, you shall never fall." (2 Peter 1:10). You shall never fall if you make it sure, but if you can be content without the assurance of election and God's love, you may fall, and for all that I know, break your necks forever, and perish forevermore.

Therefore, examine yourselves. What does your conscience tell you? You are not sure of God's favour, nor your election to life? You hope well, you say, but you are not assured of it, neither does it disturb your sleep a bit, nor hinder your sports, and your pleasures, and your mirth. It is certain you were never zealous for God. What a woeful thing is this! Have you but one soul, and are you no more careful of it? Are you to live either forever in heaven or hell, when you die, in all torture and torment world without end? And are you no more diligent to make sure beforehand? Perhaps you may be saved, yes, but perhaps you may be damned. And have you no more love for your soul than to be content with uncertainties?

Oh, how many are there among us who have no assurance from God what he means to do with them? Whether to save them, or to destroy and damn them? How many go blundering on in an uncertain opinion and conjectural hope of God's favour, and have no certainty at all of the same? How many are haunted with fears and terrors, and doubts this way, and never labour to be sure? How many have had pretty assurances a good while ago, and now they have lost them, and yet they sit idly and go dreaming on in the duties of religion, as if they could shift well enough, though they never recover again? This is no zeal: If you are zealous, you can never endure to be under uncertainties, never to be content until you have gotten the assurance of God's love.

The fourth sign of zeal towards God is gladness to further and to be furthered in the ways of God. If you are zealous, you are glad to be reproved and told of your sins; glad that the Minister should confront your corruptions and expose them in the Pulpit: as a Patient is glad that the Physician should pinpoint his ailment. When Peter encountered those three thousand in the Acts and plainly told them they were murderers of Christ, as you may read in the Chapter, the Text says they gladly received the Word (Acts 2:41). Peter laid a greater sin to their charge than we have unto yours. We have told you that some of you are adulterers, and some of you drunkards, etc., which is bad enough, and you are offended hereat; but Peter told them they were murderers of Christ, and they gladly received the Word; they were not angry with Peter but with themselves, and were glad to be told of it, a sign they were zealous. A zealous person is glad to further, and to be furthered in all goodness; glad to meet with the godly, so that he may be quickened by conversation; glad to hear news of a Sermon, so that he may attend and be edified; glad of every opportunity both of doing and receiving good; glad to attend a Sacrament which is Christ's feast; just as the good Israelites were glad at the Sacrament of the Passover, they kept that feast with great gladness (2 Chronicles 30:21). They were glad that there was one, glad that they were at it, they were very glad, says the Text. If you are zealous, you will be glad of Communion, and glad to attend it. When you have been at a Sermon, you will be glad that you were there: Oh, the Word does you such good, that you go home with all gladness of heart, yes, even though the Word contradicted your corruptions. Like the good people in Nehemiah, when they had been reproved and rebuked in the Congregation, and told of their sins, and made to cry out unto God, they went home and ate their meat with all joy, glad that they understood the words that were told them (Nehemiah 8:12). Thus you would do if you were zealous towards God; but if you go about the duties of God's worship as burdensome tasks, if you do not delight in prayer, and in hearing the Word, if you can sit wearily, and wonder when the Minister will have done, one may see it in your countance, you are not joyful to hear, this is a sign you have not one iota of zeal towards God. The poor impotent man in the Acts, when Paul was preaching, he looked so merrily and so eagerly upon him, as if he would fain have it faster than Paul could deliver, he was a faithful hearer: The same heard Paul speak, and Paul steadfastly beheld him, and perceived he had faith to be healed (Acts 14:9). He perceived he had faith, how did he perceive it? He perceived it by his countenance, he could give a shrewd guess by his looks: while Paul was preaching, he looked so cheerfully, and so eagerly upon him, as if he absorbed every point that he said. The man without doubt was zealous to hear.

The fifth sign of zeal towards God is rejoicing to see the forwardness of others: "I rejoiced greatly," says John to the elect Lady, "that I found of thy children walking in the truth" (2 John 4). Even if it may seem a slight to you that others should be as gracious and renowned as yourself, yet you will rejoice in it: it might have seemed a slight to Moses, that Eldad and Medad, of low rank in the Church, should prophesy in the Camp. Before, Moses was considered the only Prophet of the Lord, but now Eldad and Medad prophesy as well as he: this might have seemed a slight to him, yet he was so far from resenting it, that he was glad to hear it; "Would God that all the Lord's people were Prophets" (Numbers 11:29). I confess a good man may be discontented at first, even good Joshua himself had his flesh and blood stirred up at that time, "Moses, forbid them," says he. But a godly soul will check himself, and bring down his spirit, and compel his heart to be glad, and rejoice in the goodness of others, even if it seems a slight to him. A good Minister rejoices to hear of another Minister's gifts that outstrip his own. A good person rejoices to see others who are better and better loved than themselves, even if younger, inferior, and otherwise less esteemed. But if you do not rejoice to see people zealous for God, it is certain you are wretched: perhaps you think much of it, your eye is evil because they are so good and godly, and the like; this is a sign of a graceless heart: perhaps you are inclined to judge harshly of such and such because they are holier and more precise than yourself, but if you were zealous, you would rejoice to see it. If you have a better gift than another, you are obliged to help him: if he has a better gift than you, he is obliged to be helpful to you. It is a good saying of Augustine, "Take away envy, and what I have is yours: I will take away envy, and then what you have is mine." If you are zealous, you will rejoice nonetheless. Even if it's a child, you will rejoice that he is better gifted than yourself; indeed, a carnal heart may do that, and be proud, rejoicing that his child is better memorised, better-witted, better-gifted than himself. "This is my child," he thinks, "this is my son, this is my daughter, never a father or mother around here can say they have such a child." This is nothing but pride. But even if it's a servant, or even a stranger, or even someone you consider your enemy, you will rejoice in his gifts; so that God may be glorified, it matters not if I am disgraced, indeed, I count it an honour that my shame in the world may be the stirrup for God's honour to rise up. Thus you will reason, if you have a spirit of true zeal. It is greatly to be lamented how many symptoms of Atheism are among us in this regard: for men are so far from rejoicing in the progress of others, that they grumble, and they rage at nothing so much as that anyone should be eager and zealous for God; they would rather have a hundred boon-companions than one zealous man, they would rather be acquainted with twenty who are carnal than one who is holy in his ways. "I thank God," says one, "we have never a Puritan in our Parish." "I am glad we can say, we have none of these singular fellows in our town," says another. I speak not of such as the Law counts Puritans, enemies to the State and the Church, indeed, it is a blessing there are none such: but of the godly who are called Puritans by the impure tongues of the wicked; the State has no better friends under heaven, the Kingdom no better Subjects in the world, than they are: for these are they who pray away God's judgments from the Land, who earnestly pray to the Lord for the King and Council, and the Church, while the men of the world, by their drunkenness, and whoredoms, and covetousness, and security, and contempt of God's Word, are drawing down vengeance on the Nation, and provoke God to punish us. But these are they whom most people have little joy in. O my brethren, where we have ten or twenty such Puritans in our Parish, I wish to God we had a hundred. I tell you, the day will come, that the worst drunkard in the Town would give a world, if he had it, to be such a Puritan. In this sense, even the Heathen says, that every good man is a Puritan: "An entire man of life, and a pure man, pure from the sins that others do live in." If you had any zeal towards God, you would be glad that all the Country were such Puritans.

The sixth sign of zeal towards God is zeal for God's Church and his people. Paul, before his conversion, you may know his zeal was not right because his zeal was against the Church. "Concerning zeal," says he, "I persecuted the Church" (Philippians 3:6). His zeal was against the Church, and therefore not right; but after his conversion, he had a zealous care for all the Church, his zeal was then for the Church. If the Church were not well, oh how it troubled him! If the Church were well, oh how it comforted him! If the Church were anywhere persecuted or infected with error and the doctrine of devils, then he was frequent in prayer for it, often would he labour, and sigh, and mourn for it, and be writing for the good of it. Now the Saints and the people of God, these are the Church. "Unto the Churches of Galatia" (Galatians 1:2), that is, unto God's people in Galatia. "To feed the Church of God" (Acts 20:28), that is, the people of God. "Greet the Church that is in their house" (Romans 16:5), that is, the Saints that are in their house. "In all Churches of the Saints" (1 Corinthians 14:33), these are the Church of God. Now if you are zealous for God, you will be zealous for God's Church. Examine yourself. Do you mourn for the troubles and disturbances of God's Church, that the Church is so afflicted in all parts of the world? Does it prick you to the soul? Do you go to God, and put him in remembrance? "Remember the Children of Edom, O Lord, how they said, down with it, down with it, even to the ground: remember Lord the Tobiahs and Sanballat's of these times, remember Lord how they cry, down with thy people, down with them, root them out, &c." This is an infallible sign to try your heart by. If you are zealous for God, you will zealously care for the Church of God. Nehemiah cannot suppress his grief, but it would show itself in his face, even at the King's elbow, when Jerusalem lay waste.

Uriah cannot find it in his heart to eat and drink freely, or take pleasure in his own house, as long as the Ark of God, and Israel, and Judah abode in tents. You must be affected by the Church if you are zealous for God. If you are zealous for God, you must love where God loves. God loves the very gates of Zion, he loves his Church better than he loves all the world besides. And so will you, if you are zealous for him. The Church is the whole company of his Saints upon earth. One Saint is dearer than a million of other men. It is a good saying of Sirach, "One just man is better than a thousand others" (Ecclesiasticus 16:3). Though he be a beggar in the world, he is better than a thousand wicked, though they be all Lords and Nobles. Because he is one of Christ's redeemed; and so you will love him, and care for him. You will love him if you are zealous towards God, I say, you will love a child of God, even in a leathern-coat, more than father and mother, wife and children, friend or patron, so they are not Saints, I mean, with more spiritual love than you love them all. And therefore much more the Churches of the Saints.

The seventh is, If you are zealous for God, then you will be most zealous when the Lord threatens to be going away. If ever men will buy anything at the Fair, they'll buy when they are all breaking up standings, taking up their wares, and packing away. If ever they'll be forward to buy, then they will. God is now perhaps shutting up shop-doors, is now packing up his commodities, and his graces to be gone. The doors of his Sanctuary have been open a long time, and the Shop-windows of Heaven have stood wide open this many a year. And we see plainly the dead of the market is come, nobody buys almost; How long has he preached, and scarcely any converted? How many Sermons and Market-days have we had? We can hardly see one drunkard converted, one adulterer converted, one worldling converted, one unprofitable professor converted. Oh that we could see it! But alas! We cannot; our commodities stick upon our hands, we can have no vent for grace, nor Gospel, nor Christ, nor mercy, nor anything. The dead, the dead of the market beloved, the market is dead. God is now shutting up to be gone; and as we may justly fear, to remove away his Candlestick, to take away the power of his Ordinances, and to withdraw his Spirit from striving anymore with us, our stubbornness is so great. We are grown to despise his reproofs, to be incorrigible under his word, to be malicious against his rebukes, what encouragement has he to stay? Now if ever you will be zealous, now you will; now you will come in, and be wrought on, or never; now your proud hearts will stoop, or never. Now you'll cry hard, and pray hard, and beg hard, or never. "It's grievous to come a day after the Fair," as we say. I mean, now is the last pinch, in all probability it is so, either now let us look to it or never. It will be grievous to come a day after grace. No man can repent without the grace of God, and therefore if he comes a day after grace, he cannot repent, see Ezekiel 24:13.

THE TWELFTH SERMON

"Set your affections on things that are above, and not on things which are on the earth." – Colossians 3:2

I t may be asked, what means can we use to make us zealous? I answer briefly.

First, Frequent meditation. Meditate on the infinite misery you are in by nature, and because of sin; this will make you zealously humble. Meditate on your grievous iniquities by which you have dishonoured God; meditate on the immeasurable mercy of God that has not consumed you; meditate on the remarkable patience of God that has spared you thus far, not consigning you to hell; meditate on the inconceivable goodness of God in Christ, who gave up His own Son to death so that you should not perish forever. These truths are all fiery truths. When David was meditating, I cannot now recall what truths he meditated on, but it seems they were all fiery truths, igniting his soul as he pondered. "My heart was hot within me; and while I was musing, the fire kindled" (Psalm 39:3). The mere sight of a fire will warm a man a little; let your heart contemplate God and His ways, let His commandments always be in sight, and they will ignite you. Whenever you pray, meditate within yourself: "If I pray lukewarmly, God will spew me out of His mouth." Whenever you hear the Word, meditate within yourself: "I must take heed how I hear, otherwise my hearing is abominable." Whenever the Sabbath approaches, meditate within yourself: "Oh, I must consider it my delight and spend it in God's worship, both public and private, or else God will consume me." "While I was musing, the fire kindled," says the Psalmist. What's the reason you are so lukewarm in good duties? The reason is plain: you do not meditate. You may be content to hear the Word at a Sermon and let the Minister warm you for an hour; you may talk of the Word, but when you are alone, you do not meditate on it. If you would put the Law of God in your thoughts and meditate on it when you are solitary, it is a fiery law. "From his right hand went a fiery Law" (Deuteronomy 33:2). God's law is a fiery Law, and His Gospel too is a fiery Gospel; were it often in your thoughts, it would ignite you. Know this for certain: we can never have a jot of saving grace or zeal if we are not frequent in this duty. You make a god of the world if it occupies more space in your thoughts than God's word; you can never be zealous or gracious at all if you are not used to meditation. You are carnal and earthly because your thoughts are of that sort; the thoughts are incentives to vices, says Jerome, they are the incentives and bellows to kindle sin in your heart, whereas if they were heavenly, they would kindle zeal in your soul.

The second means is a constant practice of godliness. "Motus est causa caloris," says the Philosopher, "Motion is the cause of heat." Be ever in action if you would be zealous; be always engaged in the works of religion and godliness. You shall see men labouring and toiling, nearly naked in their shirts, in frost and cold, yet they are hot for all that. Labour stirs up the spirits and heats the blood; it will not allow a man to be cold. If

Peter had been rowing in his boat when he stood still in the High Priest's Hall by the chimney-corner, he would have had little need of that fire to warm him. Therefore, if you desire to be zealous, labour in reading the Scriptures, labour in hearing and applying the Word to your heart, labour in examining your conscience and repenting of your sins, and labour in praying and calling upon God. This will kindle the heat of zeal in you. "Ask, and ye shall receive, that your joy may be full" (John 16:24). Mark that, your joy may be full, your comfort may be full, your love may be full, and your hope may be full; that is, that you may be zealous, for zeal is the fullness of every affection in its kind. "Oh," says one, "I am so dull and dead. I pray indeed, but my prayers are dead; and I hear, but my hearing is dead. I see abundance of vanity in my heart, thoughts, and actions, and I am so dead. Lord, what shall I do?" Dead are you? And do you wonder you are dead? You will not labour to be quickened; you are reluctant to put in the effort to be quickened. You idly go about your work. "Otium mors est, & vivi hominis sepultura," as Seneca speaks: "Idleness is death; idleness is the burying of a man alive." You are idle and unwilling to labour with God to be quickened. When David was pondering and musing, and considering the vanity of his mind, he was as dead as a timber-log; it deadened his soul completely to see his corruptions. But what did he do? He laboured with God against it. He laboured with fasting, meditating, and praying again and again, asking the Lord to quicken him. Nine times in one Psalm, he says, "Turn away mine eyes from beholding vanity, and quicken thou me in thy way" (Psalm 119:37). "Quicken me, O Lord, according to thy Word," in one verse. "Quicken me according to thy judgments," in another verse. "Quicken thou me according to thy lovingkindness," in another verse. Again, "Quicken thou me after thy lovingkindness." "Quicken me, O Lord, according to thy Word," in another verse. He never left his heart alone until he had obtained life, spirit, and quickening again. As long as you are lazy in good duties, it's no wonder you're dead. Labouring and striving in good exercises will warm a man's soul and make it more zealous.

The third means is keeping good company, as Cleopas was heated by being in Christ's company. "Did not our hearts burn within us," says he, "while he talked with us on the way?" (Luke 24:32). As the bawdy Poet said of his sweetheart, "Accede ad ignem hanc," "Come to this fire": a whore inflames an adulterer; one wicked man heats another unto lust and sin. So every child of God is a fire to heat you. Would you be zealous? Associate with God's people; keep company with the Saints and those who excel in grace and virtue. "Two are better than one, for if they fall, the one will lift up his fellow; but woe to him that is alone when he falleth, for he hath not another to help him up" (Ecclesiastes 4:9-11). "Again, if two lie together, then they have heat, but how can one be warm alone?" (Ecclesiastes 4:11). Do you complain, "I have no zeal; I would be glad to be zealous, but I am exceedingly lukewarm; no matter what I do, I remain the same"? Alas! Do you ever expect to be otherwise as long as you keep company with vain persons? They may talk of heaven now and then, but there is no heat or warmth in their speeches; they are dead-hearted themselves, and so are their speeches—dead and lifeless. "Oh, but I live in a place that is wicked, and there's scarcely one godly person in the house where I dwell, and I can find none to warm me." Do you? So did Obadiah in Ahab's Court. There was never a good Courtier to converse with, and therefore what did he do? He made use of God's Prophets in private (1 Kings 18:4). Though he might not be seen in their company for fear of losing their lives, he hid them in a cave and there sought their company in secret. If you neglect the society of the Saints, never expect to be zealous. Thomas was very faithless and full of his doubts; one reason was this:

the Disciples of Christ had meetings together, and Thomas was not with them (John 20:24). The coals that lie together in the hearth glow and are fired, while the little coals that fall off and lie separately are black without fire. If you ever desire to be zealous, value the fellowship of the Saints. You can hardly come where two or three Saints are gathered together, but you shall find Christ in the midst of them.

The fourth means is shunning the occasions of sin. Moses would not leave so much as a hoof behind him in Egypt (Exodus 10:26) so that there might be no occasion for the people to turn back into Egypt. If he had left even a hoof behind, that would have been an occasion to go there to fetch it. Abraham would not take so much as a thread or a shoelatchet from the King of Sodom when offered, lest there should be any hint to the flesh to distrust God. You can never be zealous unless you shun the occasions of sin. If the heart has even a single occasion to be vain, it's highly likely it will become so; deadness will creep in upon the slightest occasion. Give a thief even a chance of getting something, and his fingers cannot resist. When David gave occasion to the enemies of the Lord to blaspheme, the Lord told him he would punish him (2 Samuel 12:14). Why? Because if they had even the slightest occasion, they would be sure to take it. Let no one put an occasion to fall in his brother's way (Romans 14:13). Alas! If the flesh has no occasion, it will seize one; it's not enough to keep out of sin, but you must also keep far from all occasions of sin. "Keep thee far from a false matter" (Exodus 23:7). One might think, "I may go so far and not sin. Thus far I may go, and so far is this lawful." But let me tell you, if you go that far, your own heart will find an occasion to go further, and then you are undone. "Nimiâ licentiâ sumus omnes deteriores," says Terence. We are all worse for taking too much liberty; if it once becomes an occasion to the flesh, you are lost. Zeal cannot tolerate the occasions of evil; even the slightest occasions will smother it.

The fifth means is to eschew the beginnings of sin. Peter did but begin to rebuke Christ, saying, "Master, spare thyself," and Christ so detested the very beginnings of that sin that he said, "Get thee behind me, Satan" (Matthew 16:22). The devil was in that beginning of sin. The Scribes and the Pharisees began to reason, saying, "Who is this that speaks blasphemies?" and Jesus condemned these beginnings of reasonings (Luke 5:21). Those invited to the Feast in the Gospel did not come but made excuses and were cast into utter darkness for their labour. But how did they fall into that sin? The Scripture plainly shows, because they did not eschew the beginnings of the sin; they all with one consent began to make excuses (Luke 14:18). "Principiis obsta," set yourself against the beginning of sin; if you allow your heart to begin once, it will surely go further. The Spirit of God uses a good phrase, "fall into sin." He that stands, let him take heed lest he fall: a man standing on a high rock, if he does not look to the beginning of his fall, cannot stop himself until he has completely fallen to the bottom. If by chance he catches hold somewhere, which is highly unlikely, if he does not, I say, it's a wonder if he does not break his neck. You can never have the life of grace in you unless you take heed of the beginnings of sin.

Be exhorted, all of you who would fear God, to be zealous.

First, consider, you can never be revenged on your worst enemies unless you are zealous. You would be glad to be revenged on your sworn enemies. Samson begged hard of the Lord that he might be revenged on the Philistines for his two eyes, but you have worse enemies than the Philistines were to him. Sin, the World, the Flesh, and the Devil—these are the worst enemies that any mortal man has. It's good to be revenged on them. You can never be revenged on them unless you are zealous; there is no enemy besides that it is lawful to be revenged on, but only on these. You can lawfully be revenged on these; they have done you much harm, brought you into the state of wrath and damnation, made you accursed, and liable to hell-torments forever. They have plucked out the two eyes of your soul. Now, if you would be zealous, you may be revenged on them. The Apostle puts zeal and revenge together, "Yea, what zeal, yea, what revenge" (2 Corinthians 7:11). If you are zealous, you may be revenged on sin that has done you so much mischief. It has troubled your peace, defiled your conscience, disabled you from worshipping God, and hindered many good things from you. You have had no hurt, sorrow, or evil but you may thank sin for it. You have just cause to be revenged on sin; there is an inbred desire of revenge in a man upon those who wrong him. The heathen could say,

"Est vindicta bonum vitâ jucundius ipsâ."

Revenge is sweeter than life itself: Here it is true, and nowhere else. All other revenge is a damnable premunire against God; "vengeance is mine," says he, "and who is he that revengeth himself" to intrench upon God's right? But here revenge is commanded, yea, it's sweeter than life: here revenge and spare not, and this is the way: get zeal, and be as hot as a furnace in anger against sin, and beat it as Moses did the Israelites' calf, into dust and powder. Has your filthy cozening heart deceived you so often? Hereby you may be revenged on it; be zealous to search it, and curb it, and tame it; have your lusts been greedy, proud, and sensual? This humour they must have, and this fashion they must follow, and this pleasure they must take, and this liberty they must use. Oh, if you would be zealous, you may easily be revenged on your lusts; hereby you may be revenged on the devil, and spite his kingdom to advance Christ's; hereby you may be revenged on your flesh, that has played the traitor so often with you; you may afflict it, and master it, and block it, and subdue it; hereby you may trample upon the world, that has so often ensnared you; you may scorn it and contemn it, and all the glory of it, and count it as dross and dung in comparison to Christ; hereby you may trample Satan under your feet. It is a strange thing how little men study to be revenged on these enemies; let our own brother give us but a cross word, we are at daggers drawn to be revenged; but the devil may baffle us, and the devil may tempt us, and beguile us, we put it all up. Let a servant but anger us a little, and offend us but in a piece of service, or an errand; oh, we are so revengeful, and ready to make them smart for it! But sin may cross us in our souls, and rob us of Christ, and deprive us of grace, and mercy, and peace, and all; yet we are good friends with it, we take nothing amiss; alas! These men are monsters and mad men. One day you shall see that sin, and your lust, and Satan, whose temptations you have been led by, etc., they are the worst enemies in the world; and if ever you desire to be revenged upon them, oh, endeavour to be zealous.

Secondly, consider, you will never be able to do good unto others unless you be zealous. When men go dreamingly on in Religion, they can never do good upon others: what do others think? They think basely and meanly thereof, as if it were a matter of nothing; but when they see a man zealous, this affects them indeed, if anything will do it. When a man is zealous at a game, he laughs exceedingly, he is as merry as he can stand on his legs; another man that shall see it, will be apt to demand what fine merry pleasant game is that? So it is with ambitious men, when a man is zealous for a living, he rides through thick and thin, through frost and snow all the night long, he seeks this friend and that Noble man to help him in his suit; what will folks say? Certainly, he is going about some great living or other, he is so eager about it. So if you would be zealous for God, and fervent in religion, men would be compelled to conceive better of godliness, and of Christ, than you might provoke others to godliness. Zeal is a provoking grace. "Your zeal hath provoked very many" (2 Corinthians 9:2). As zeal in charity provokes, so does zeal in every good work provoke. Where Theodoret observes the wisdom of Paul, for he provokes the Macedonians by the zeal of the Corinthians, and the Corinthians by the zeal of the Macedonians; for zeal does mutually provoke one another. Oh, what a deal of good might you do in the house where you dwell, in the Parish where you live, in the Country where you are, if you would labour to be zealous! I knew an old man, whether he be dead now or alive, I know not, that used constantly to go to the labouring men in the field, and catechize them, and pose them in Religion, as they were reaping and working; he would go to men's shops where he was acquainted, and stir them up to have care of their souls, and by this means brought above forty men and women to seek out for Heaven, that before had no more care that way, then if they had been like a company of beasts. Wouldn't you be glad to do good? You will never be able to do it unless you are zealous. Paul had women, and sundry private Christians, that are said to labour with him in the Gospel. This, beloved, would cause Religion to thrive here among us.

Thirdly, consider, I pray you, that you will discourage us who are God's Ministers, unless you are zealous. If men would be zealous in hearing and zealous in proficience, it would make us go cheerfully on in our callings. When Titus told Paul the fervent mind of the Corinthians, it encouraged the Apostle; "when he told us your fervent mind, we rejoiced the more" (2 Corinthians 7:7). So it is in the Original, when he told us your zeal. Saint Paul was cheered to hear that. What greater discouragement to a Schoolmaster than that his scholars should be dull and not profit? What greater disheartening to a Captain than that his soldiers should be fainthearted and without life? And what greater grief to a Minister than that his people should be senseless and lifeless? It made Jeremiah weary of his life; it made the Prophet Micah lament bitterly. "Woe is me, I am like the Grape gleaners." It made the Prophet Isaiah cry out, "I have labored in vain." On the contrary, when the people are zealous and forward, and drink in the words of eternal life with all greediness, and bring forth fruit with abundance, this makes a Minister go merrily on in his function. Zelo Ecclesia Dei congregatur, says Saint Ambrose: It is zeal that does gather a Church, the zeal of the Minister, and the zeal of the people; the Lord quicken us in his mercy, that we may encourage one another daily. Let us be encouraged by you; when you are reproved, be not offended. You think the Minister spites you; alas! We have no reason to wish any of your fingers to ache, much less to wish that your souls should perish. When Saint Paul commanded that the incestuous Corinthian should be delivered to Satan, did he wish him any hurt? No, 'Deliver him unto Satan,' says he, 'for the destruction of the flesh, that the spirit may be saved in the day of the Lord Jesus' (1 Corinthians 5:5), ὥστε τὸ πνεῦμα σωθῆναι, etc., says Chrysostom. 'No mortal man loved that offender in Corinth more than Paul did,' says he, 'when he would have him delivered unto Satan.' It was only that he might know he was a damned wretch, unless he amended, and that the devil should have him unless he were humbled. What was his reason? His reason was this, that his soul might be saved in that day. "O the Minister preaches damnation so often, he is unmerciful to our souls." "O my brethren, we intend you the greatest mercies of heaven in so saying; it is that you may not run into damnation, but may repent and believe the Gospel." Do not thus discourage us whom God has sent to you as his Ministers to labour in the word and doctrine among you, but stir up yourselves to be zealous in hearing and obeying, that we may give up an account of your souls unto God with all cheerfulness.

Fourthly, consider, you can never be excellent if you are not zealous. A Christian should strive to excel: aut Caesar, aut nullus; nothing but the best should suffice a Christian. Would you then be excellent? Get this same zeal: zeal runs after the best things, "Covet earnestly the best gifts" (1 Corinthians 12:31). The Word in the Original is ζηλοῦτε, be zealous after the best things. Would you be excellent in prayer, and excellent in the duties of religion? Be zealous therein. A Christian is like fire: fire mounts up absolutely aloft and ascends above all. So does a Christian: he is better than all the men of this world put them all together: like Job, there is none like him in all the earth. Every man else fain would be excellent; a worldling strives to excel others in wealth, a politician to excel others in wisdom, a scholar to excel others in learning, a tradesman to excel others in his profession. He is of a base spirit that does not desire to excel in something; and shall not a Christian then desire to excel in grace?

Fifthly, consider, I pray, who you may be like if once you are zealous; you may be like unto the Angels of heaven, "they are spirits and flaming fire," says the Apostle (Hebrews 1:7). If you are zealous for God, you are a bodily Seraphim; though you can never be without sin as long as you live in this world, yet as Gregory speaks, "in the mouth of zeal you may swallow up your sins; nothing will devour and consume sin so well as true zeal." O get a coal of this fire then from God's Altar, and heat your heart with it, and while you may be like the blessed Angels of God, be not like the brutish sons of the old Adam. Zeal is it that makes an Angel to be an Angel. "Angeli sine zelo nihil sunt," says Ambrose, "the Angels are nothing without zeal." If you had zeal unto God, then you might be like unto Angels.

Sixthly, consider what infinite need you have of true zeal. Suppose a great frost and a tedious cold winter were coming, and then no fuel were to be had. Would not men buy as much fuel as they could get, stack it, and store it, so they might have it when needed? Otherwise, they would not be able to live or to prepare their sustenance; they would surely starve without fuel in such a cold time. Beloved, I speak to those who have ears to hear. There's a cold time of religion coming, and the wrath of God is ready to break forth, to plague men's souls with icy coldness because they have despised the zeal of the Lord, and there will be no fuel to be had then. God knows how soon the power of God's Word may be taken from us. You who love your own souls, look around, lay up some fuel, and be not slothful in all this business. Do all diligence to store up grace for yourselves; this will help you to zeal. "Not slothful in business, fervent in spirit" (Romans 12:11). ζῆλοι, so it is in the Original, zealous in spirit. If you will not be slothful in business, you shall quickly be zealous in spirit. O get quickly the spirit of prayer, to be zealous in prayer by faith; it will be the best string to your bow, it will be your only thing left. Nothing left for you but prayer in secret unto God. Do you not need to be diligent for that? When a poor cripple has nothing to trust to but only his begging, he will ply that. When a poor day-labourer has never a foot of ground nor anything but only his fingers' end to maintain him and his family, he will be sure to employ them. Alas, if he should have a wound in his hands, or he should lose the use of his fingers, what shall he do? When a man's house leans mainly upon one pillar, he will look to that pillar. Thus it is with you. You shall have little else besides prayer; you must get it out of your fingers' ends. Now we, who are God's Ministers, study all the week long to quicken you here when you come to God's House, while you are thinking of other matters. But if God should once take us away from you, all the work lies upon your backs, and you have little else besides Prayer and God's Word to help you. O, therefore, be not slothful in this business, get a sure hold in Christ, that you may be able to hold in the evil day. No matter though the world deride you; for if you have true zeal, says Chrysostom, you will fear praise or dispraise no more than if you were all alone in the world, and no man beside you. If no persuasions can prevail with you to trade for this zeal that I speak of, hear what the Lord Jesus does peremptorily threaten: "It shall come to pass that I will spew thee out of my mouth."

The Thirteenth Sermon

"Set your affections on things that are above, and not on things which are on the earth." – Colossians 3:2

Hitherto I have shown how the affections must be set upon God, and especially the zeal of them. I have shown the woeful estate of that soul that does not set its affections this way, together with sundry uses of the point. Now let me persuade you with motives to this duty, namely, to set your affections on God. The Apostle in this place uses five strong persuasions hereto, as the words may also be construed.

First, by a strong obtestation, as a mother persuades her child, as ever thou art my child do this for me. If ye then be risen with Christ, seek those things that are above: If ye be risen with Christ, set your affection on things above, as ever ye be risen with Christ, do it, as he beseeches the Philippians. If there be therefore any consolation in Christ, if any comfort of love, if any fellowship of the Spirit, if any bowels and mercies, fulfil ye my joy, Phil. 2:1, 2. q. d. as ever ye acknowledge any comfort in Christ, as ever ye believe any communion of the Holy Ghost, any mercies and bowels in God, fulfil this exhortation: this is a strong persuasion indeed, for if this cannot prevail with you, ye deny all the comforts of Christ, ye deny all communion of the Spirit, ye deny all the mercies of God, and therefore it is strong; as a mother counts it a strong entreaty to her child; as ever thou art my child, as ever thou takest me to be thy mother, obey me in this; for if her child will not yield, he must needs deny the womb that bare him, and the paps that gave him suck. Wilt thou deny the Lord Jesus? Wilt thou deny his resurrection, and all interest in it? If thou wilt not deny it, set thine affections on God, as ever thou art risen with Christ, be sure for to do it. Wilt thou set thine affections upon the things of this world, when Christ entreats thee as ever thou art his, to set thine affections on him?

Secondly, The Apostle here persuades by a strong argumentation; for ye are dead, says he, verse 3. Set your affections on things above, not on things on the earth, for ye are dead, ye are dead to the things of this life; will ye set your affections to those things ye are dead to? Ye are dead to the things of this life, if ye be Christ's, and therefore set not your affections on them; mortui non mordent, as we say, dead men bite not one another with slanders and reproaches; did ye ever see a dead man go up and down drinking and carousing, whoring and gaming, and worrying and fretting? I will as soon believe that a dead man can do this, as a true Christian. I confess that corruption may carry a good Christian into sin, but he is dead to these courses, he cannot set his affections hereon, he is dead; and will ye set your affections on the things of this world, now ye are dead? Bring a child of God to your drinkings, and your carousings, his affections are dead, he hath no heart to them: bring him to your sportings, and your vain merriments, and your fooleries, you shall see him so dead to them, that ye shall have no delight in his company. S. Paul makes this an argument ab absurdo. How shall we that are dead to sin, live any longer therein? Rom. 6:2. How is this possible? I shall as soon believe it, as that a dead man should walk along your streets in a winding-sheet: What? Know you not this, says he, what a Christian, and yet his affections on such courses as these? This is impossible, how shall ye? So that this is another strong persuasion, because ye are dead, therefore set not your affections below.

Thirdly, the Apostle here persuades by a strong reason: Christ is your life, ver. 4. Life is sweet, it is true, and a person's affections are strong for their life. "Vestes ac omnia vendes," thou wilt part with clothes, and part with money, and part with lands, and part with all for thy life: thine affections are strongly set to life. Now Christ is thy life, or else thou art but a damned wretch: if thou art a true Christian, Christ is thy life, and wilt not thou set thine affections on thy life? His Commandments are thy life, his Word is thy life, his ordinances are thy life, his promises, his favours, his blood, are thy life, and wilt thou not set thine affections on thy life? If thou art a true Christian, thou wilt pray for life, and repent for life, and sanctify the Sabbath for life, and put up an injury, and be obedient to God for life, all thine affections conspire together for life: thou lovest thy life and thou desirest thy life, and thou rejoicest in thy life, and thou fearest that which is hurtful to life, and hatest that which is contrary to life, all thine affections will be to thy life; and therefore set thine affections on Christ, for he is thy life.

Fourthly, the Apostle here persuades by a strong deduction. When Christ shall appear, then ye also shall appear with him in glory, ver. 4. This is an excellent motive to set thine affections on God, because he will bring thee to glory; every person affects glory. Now all the glory of this world is a blaze, as our Proverb is, a good Proverb it is, it is but a blaze, and not worthy thine affections, none but base hearts will affect this; thou art the child of wrath and damnation from the cradle to the coffin, thou art going to hell and confusion, if thou art not a new creature in Christ: and wilt thou affect to be a Gentleman, affect to be a Knight or a Lord? Wilt thou affect to get credit and honour, and repute among people, to be praised by men's mouths? This is even as if a thief should affect credit as he is going to the gallows. Set thine affections then upon God and upon Christ, when he appears he will help thee to a kingdom of glory. Christ is the King of glory; Who is the King of glory? It is the Lord of hosts, he is the King of glory; set thine affections on him then. The vulgar have a pretty saying, "He that is in favour with the King, is half a King." What may not such an one do, what may not such an one have, if he be in favour with a King? "Potens potentum amicitia," Potent is the favour that a person hath with him that is potent. And therefore set thine affections upon Christ, let thine affections be in favour with Christ; what is it then thou canst not have? Thine affections are potent, if they are in favour with him; all power is given to me in heaven and earth, says Christ, Mat. 28:18. Christ is very potent: if thine affections are not set on him, he is potent enough to damn thee; if they are, he is potent to save thee, and when he appears, then shalt thou appear with him in glory.

Fifthly, the Apostle here persuades by a strong illation or inference: Mortify therefore, says he, mortify your earthly members, inordinate affection, &c. verse. 5. Mark, he calls the affection, when it is not set aright upon God, he calls it inordinate affection; if thine affections run more after the things of this life, than after Christ and his Word, and his Commandments, and his Ordinances, thine affections are disorderly, they are all out of order. Order is to be observed in all things, and wilt thou suffer disorder to break in upon thy soul? Disorder turns all topsy-turvy; disorder will undo a whole Kingdom: if a Kingdom is out of order, it must needs go to wrack. If a family is out of order, it must needs be brought to naught; nothing can stand without order, no art can consist without order: and certainly thy soul cannot stand without order; if thine affections are out of order, thy soul is in civil wars, and cannot stand but must perish. Now if thine affections are not set upon God, they are all out of order. What's the reason that people are so forgetful of their souls? If their bellies hunger, they remember to fill them; if their backs are naked, they remember to clothe them; if their markets are not made, they remember to dispatch them; but their souls may perish and be damned, they do not remember them: What's the reason of this? Their affections are out of order. "Ordo est mater memoriae," Order is the mother of memory; a person can never remember their businesses, if all is out of order. Saint Paul rejoiced to behold their order in Colossae, Col. 2:5. he was glad to see that all their affairs were in order, why? Then he hoped all would go well with them: David prays God to order his steps: "Order my steps in thy Word, and let not any iniquity have dominion over me," Psa. 119:133. He knew that his lusts would be like masterless hounds, he should have no hope with them, if his soul were out of order. "Order my steps in thy word," says he, "and let not any iniquity have dominion over me." If thine affections are out of order, alas, every lust will domineer, every corruption will be like a masterless hound, as we say. Job says, that death is out of order, Job 10:22. And Aquinas and other Divines thence do observe, that hell is out of order; and wilt thou suffer a disorder to come among thine affections? Alas, they will be so busy about the things of this life, that thou shalt find no while for better employments, no while for repentance and amendment, no while for bethinking thyself of thy ways to provide for thy soul. Disordered persons are busybodies, says the Text. "We hear there be some among you that walk disorderly among you, and are busy-bodies," 2 Th. 3:11. If thine affections are disorderly, they will be so busy, that thou shalt never find leisure to traffic for Heaven, or the salvation of thy soul. Beloved, this must needs then be a strong persuasion to set your affections above, because otherwise thine affections are all out of order. Thus far the Apostle here helps us with motives expressed in the context.

That which the Apostle begins, let the theme of my Text go further in the same. Many and sweet motives there are that we may be stirred up to this duty by, to set our affections on God.

The first motive is taken from the easiness that our affections put us in to prosecute anything we affect: if our affections be set on a thing, they make it easy to prosecute; if thou affect the things of the world, thine affections make it easy to labour and to toil, easy to rise early, easy to sit up late, easy to travel, and go through any other difficulty: the covetous man thinks his labour to be easy, so he may gain and get profit; the voluptuous man thinks it easy to hunt and to hawk, and ride himself out of breath, so he may have pleasure and delight. "Take thine ease," says the rich man in the Gospel, "take thine ease, eat, drink, and be merry," Luk. 12:19. He thought it easy to pull down, and to build up, easy to gather in his harvests and his wealth, easy to be an Epicure and a drunkard, and voluptuous, why? Because his affections were set hereupon: is it so that thine affections are able to make any business easy, O set thine affections upon God, repentance will be easy, mortification will be easy, and self-denial will be easy, and to suffer all the reproaches of Christ will be easy, if once thine affections were settled that way; knowledge is easy to him that understandeth, Prov. 14 6. "The scorner seeks it," says Solomon, "and he cannot find it; the worldling seeks it and he cannot find it; it is hard," says one, "to know how to pray and be holy, it is hard," says another, "to know how to repent and give over my sins, and be strict, and I cannot do it." No? That is, because thine affections are bent another way? But if thine affections were set upon Heaven, this knowledge were easy. "Come unto me ye that labour," says the world,

"I will make it easy to travel, and cark, and care; come unto me," says pleasure, "I will make it easy to be merry and to laugh: come unto me," says the flesh, "I will make it easy to be revenged on him that does wrong thee; I will make it easy to obtain this and that." So says the Lord Jesus, "Come unto me ye that labour, and I will give you rest, my yoke is easy," Mat. 11:30. Whatever thou affectest, come to it, and thou shalt find it to be easy. A man would wonder how the labouring man will sweat and work till he is faint, to get a little maintenance, the reason is this, he affects it. One would wonder what dangers Alexander did run through, to enlarge his kingdom and his power, the reason is this, he affects it. One would wonder how Baal's Priests cut themselves after their manner with knives and with lancers, till the blood gushed out upon them, 1 Kin. 18:28. the reason was this, they affected will-worship. Anything is easy when a man does affect it: wouldst thou persuade a man to any hardship under heaven? Do but turn his affections unto it, and thou hast prevailed: "Flectere est victoriae," says Austin, do but bend a man's affections, and thou hast prevailed with him. O sayst thou, I find it so hard to be heavenly, so hard to be zealous, so hard to depend upon God; what is the reason of this? Thine affections are earthly; if thine affections were set right, it would be the easiest of ten thousand. "My heart hath such a haunt, and I find it so hard to break myself of it; I am choleric, and I find it so hard for to bridle it; I am poor and afflicted, and I find it so hard for to bear it; alas, alas, it is the easiest thing in the world, if thine affections were to it." Wouldest thou not be glad to count it to be easy to serve God, easy to walk in all holiness; no such treasure as to live at ease, as we say. I know thou wouldest be glad to find it easy to abandon thy corruptions, and please God better than thou dost, O labour then to set thine affections on God, and all things are easy. Should we persuade thee to part with thy geegaws, thou art so loath, it is a hard task to persuade thee, that is, because thou wilt be proud still: should we persuade thee to discard wicked company out of thy house, thou keepest an Alehouse, and thou art loath to thrust them forth of thy house, that is, because thou wouldest fain have their custom, thine affections are that way, and therefore it is not easy to persuade thee, but set thine affections aright, and every difficulty is easy.

The second motive is taken from the shamelessness of the affections: If thou beest once deeply affected with anything, thou wilt never be ashamed of it. See a proud fantastical fool that affecteth his long locks, and his lovelock. Everyone that is sober-minded and sees him, is ready to say, "What a humerous fool is yonder man, what a ruffian he is! How like a Mastiff or a Bedlam does he look!" Yet the fool is not ashamed thereof, because he affects it. See a light-headed wretch that is ever a fooling, and ever a jesting, and ever a toying, and playing, and this sport, and that sport. Every grave man that beholds him is apt to say, "What a vain man is this? I never saw such a light-headed sot in my life;" yet the wretch is not ashamed thereof, because he affects it. The swearer swears, and is not ashamed: the worldling covets, and is not ashamed; the mocker mocks, and is not ashamed; though every man in his wits that does view them, marvels at their madness, and how desperate they be: all cry shame on them, yet they are not ashamed because they affect it. "Thou hast a whore's forehead, thou refusest to be ashamed," Jer. 3:3. The whore whose affections are set on her lovers, and her adulterers, cannot be ashamed, but she dares go on for all the shame of the earth; why? Because she affects them. Nero was not ashamed of his villainies in the open market of Rome. Vespasian was not ashamed of his stinking covetousness by urine. If it be thus, O why dost thou not set thine affections on God, and on Christ, and his laws? Thou couldst never be ashamed hereof, if once thou didst truly affect them. When David's affections were stirred to dance before the Ark of God, and put off his garment to do it the better, "Fie upon thee, fie upon thee," says Micol "Fie for shame, what art thou not ashamed to make thyself vile on this fashion?" "I will be more vile yet," says he, "If this be vileness, to rejoice before God, if this be esteemed a vileness, I will be more vile yet:" he could not be ashamed, because his affections were set upon God's Ark. "Out you Puritan, you are a vile companion, to be so precise as you are; you must be reproving and talking of the Scripture upon every occasion, out you hypocrite you, are you not ashamed to do thus?" "No, no," he is not ashamed, he can never be ashamed: if this be to be a Puritan, to be holy and strict against sin, "I will be more a Puritan yet; If this be to be an hypocrite, to be labouring to draw others from their lusts, I will be a more hypocrite yet. If this be singularity, not to do as the men of this world do, I will be more singular yet; I will speak of God's testimonies and it were before Kings; and I will not be ashamed," Psal. 119:46. Impudence, and not to be ashamed, is a very great matter; if it be in sin, it is desperate, it is a sign a man is desperately affected towards sin; but if it be in good, it is admirable; it is a holy kind of impudence, it is a sign a man is deeply affected towards good, so affected that nothing can make him ashamed. Never will a man be ashamed of that which he affects; "Fie for shame, will you be rich and take in such profits? Will you be in such credit? Fie, will you be a Lord and a Nobleman in such honour? Will you be learned and gather so much knowledge?" He conceives they are all fools that say so, though peradventure they do not affect such things, yet he does, and therefore he will not be ashamed of them. So if thine affections be set upon Christ, thou wilt never be ashamed of his cross, never ashamed of his badge, never ashamed of his Word. The children of the devil are not ashamed of their abominations; they can drink and be drunken, and vomit, and reel, and not be ashamed; they can be proud and carnal, and have no more religion in them than the stock, and not be ashamed. Agesilaus will not be ashamed of his halting, Philopaemenes will not be ashamed of his deformity, when they hold it their credit to be thus as they were. O therefore set thine affections on God, and thou shalt never be ashamed of his ways.

The third motive is taken from the hankeringness of the affections. Look at what thou settest thine affections upon, that thou wilt hanker after. If thou set thine affections on the things of this life, thy heart will so hanker after them, that they will haunt thee whatever thou goest about; they will haunt thee at prayer time, and haunt thee at Church time, they will haunt thee on the Sabbath, and haunt thee at the Sacrament; like the Fly in Albertus, that was ever hankering after the bald head: though he flapped it off again and again, yet still it would be hankering, he could never be rid of it, it would still be hankering. Who would be thus troubled with his affections? He cannot go by an Alehouse, but his affections water to go in: he cannot see a pair of Tables, but his affections hanker after a game: he cannot meet with an injury, but his affections itch to revenge; he cannot speak well nor do anything which is commendable, but his affections must be swelling with pride. Who, I say, would be thus troubled with his affections? Though God had forbidden Lot's wife to look back upon pain of his heavy displeasure, nevertheless her affections did so hanker after her house, and her country, and her ancient acquaintance, that she looked behind her, Gen. 19:26. Her carnal affections did so haunt her every step she took, that they never lind till she looked back. "They are greedy dogs, they look to their own way," Isa. 56:11. Thine affections if they be not set right, they are like greedy dogs in the Kitchen, that are ever looking to the platters, be the Mistress's eye never so little off, they are licking instantly. So thine affections are ever hankering after that which thou affectest: and therefore thou art best to

set thine affections on God: for look where they are set, there they will
be hankering. If ever thy heart be turned to God, and thine affections
converted to him, they will ever be hankering and looking after God. "At
that day shall a man look to his maker, and his eyes shall have respect
to the holy one of Israel," Isa. 17:7. At that day, that is, when God shall
convert them, then their hearts shall ever be hankering and looking after
God. O then set thine affections on God, if thou desirest thy heart should
hanker after God. Thou art yet no better than a wretch, till thus it be
with thee. If thine affections be ever hankering after thy pleasures and
thy companions, and thy vanities, thou art never well but when thou art
at them. The Sermon is quickly tedious, and prayer tedious, and godly
discourses are tedious unto thee: why? Because thy mind hankers about
other gates matters; as long as it is thus thou canst not be saved. "Look
unto me," says Christ, "and be ye saved all the ends of the earth," Isa.
45:22. Ye can never be saved, unless ye hanker and look after me, says
the Lord; as the Heliotrope or the turn-sol that ever looks towards the
Sun, so a gracious heart does after the Lord. God counts it an honour
unto him, that the soul should be ever hankering and ever looking after
him; "Aestimari nos putamus toties, quoties aspici," says Seneca; it is
a true saying; we think we are esteemed when men do look after us;
So God counts it an honour to his Majesty, when our souls do hanker
and look after him. It is true, the things of this life may chance to draw
away our minds now and then, and make us look after them: but if we
have any grace, so much as a grain of mustard-seed, our souls will ever
be hankering and looking after God. So it was with Jonah, though his
corruptions had made him look off from God, nevertheless he could not
abide to be in that case, his heart is again looking and hankering after
God: oh for the light of his countenance, oh for his grace and his Spirit,
oh for power and strength yet to be resolute for God, "Yet will I look again

towards thy holy Temple," Jonah 2:4. Let God afflict me, I cannot but look to him; let God fling me into the Whale's belly, I cannot but hanker after him, let him cast me into the belly of hell, yet will I look again says he: his affections were set upon God, and therefore did his heart ever hanker and look after God. This is a sweet motive to persuade us: if we would once set our affections on God, our souls would ever hanker and look after God.

The fourth motive is taken from the spurrings of the affections, they spur a man to that he affects: they are animi calcaria, as Melancthon does call them, they are as it were the spurs of the soul. What is the reason that men go on in any business like lazy jaded Asses, says Vives, because they have no affection to it. What is the reason they go so sluggishly on to good duties, they sit so senselessly still in seats at a Sermon, they kneel so lumpishly and dead-heartedly in prayer to God? Because they have no spurs in their sides, they have no affection to these things. Now if we would set our affections on God, we would feel in our bosoms a certain spur that spurs us to every good word and work? A gracious heart is said to stir up itself, Exod. 36:2. God counts those prayers no prayers, that are not full of these spurrings and stirrings; there is none that calleth upon thy name, that stirreth up himself to take hold on thee. Isa. 64:7. Dost thou call upon God, and hast thou no spurrings nor stirrings in the duty? Dost thou not spur up thyself to pray with good life? The Lord says thou dost not call upon his name at all. As ever thou desirest to be stirred up and spurred on to good exercises, set thine affections on God, they are the spurs of the soul: the soul goes cheerfully on, when it goes with affection.

The fifth motive is taken from the heartiness of the affections; and therefore the heart is many times and often in Scripture put for the affections. "My heart," says Deborah, "is towards the Governors of Israel," Jud. 5.9, that is, mine affection is towards them. "O ye Corinthians, our mouth is open unto you, our heart is enlarged," 2 Cor. 6.11, that is, our affections are enlarged. Look whatever thou affectest, thy heart is set upon it; this motive is strong to persuade, for if the affections be in a manner the very heart of the soul, this may well move us to set our affections upon God; wilt thou settle thy heart anywhere else but only upon God? O how heinously does the Lord take it at thy hands, that thou hast no more heart unto him? He gives thee his Word, and thou hast no heart to it; he gives thee his Sabbath, and thou hast no heart to it; he gives thee his Sacrament, and his Ordinances, and his Sanctuary, and his Commandments, and thou hast no heart to them. O the Lord is so angry with thy soul, that he calls thee a fool and a sot, and he repents that ever he hath vouchsafed these things to such wretches as thou art. "Wherefore is there a price in the hand of a fool to get wisdom, seeing he hath no heart to it?" Prov. 17.16. Wherefore, says God, and to what end is a price put into your hand to get wisdom? Ye might have gotten wisdom a long time or ere now, how to be new creatures and in Christ, how to get grace, and peace, and mercy with God; ye have had abundance of prices put into your hands, a price of abundance of Sacraments, and Sabbaths, a price of abundance of Sermons and exhortations, many mercies and favours, many threatenings and warnings, health, strength, life, liberty; ye have had a fair time to get grace and holiness in Jesus Christ; prices have been put into your hands, but ye have had no heart nor affection to them. The Lord is exceedingly wroth with you, he casts the fool in your face, and repents that ever he hath lent you these things; wherefore is a price put into the hand of a fool, seeing he hath no heart to it? No heart nor affection to make use of it? Wherefore? Says he, to what end? Wherefore is a price put into a fool's hand, that sees not the worth of it? Better he had been sent to hell quick and never heard Sermon: better he had been damned many years since and never had the means. What, will ye be drunkards in spite of preaching? And adulterers, and fornicators, in spite of God's threats? Mockers and despisers of them that are good, lovers of pleasures more than lovers of God, in spite of the Lord Jesus? O this does woefully provoke God, that ye should have no more heart nor affection to these things than ye have. Set your affections then upon God, if ever ye will be wise to escape the vengeance to come; your affections are your heart, be not so rebellious as to deny your heart unto God.

The sixth motive is taken from the softness of the affections; the affections are the softness of the heart. "Affectus sunt foemineus animae partus," says the Philosopher, they are the feminine and softly brood of the heart. The heart is a soft heart where thine affections do stand; if thine affections be set upon the things of this life, thy heart is a soft heart thereunto, thy heart is sensible of every profit, sensible of every vain pleasure: the things of this life can easily sink down into thy heart, if thine affections be to them. O let thine affections then be set upon God: what wilt thou have a soft heart to the world, the things of the world may easily work on it? And wilt thou have a hard heart to God, that he may not work on it?

Hardness of heart is an argument that a man is damnably and desperately impudent, and will neither obey God nor his Ministers. So God tells Ezekiel the house of Israel will not hearken to thee, says he, for they will not hearken unto me; for all the house of Israel are impudent and hard-hearted, Ezek. 3.7. When their hearts were once hardened, they were so impudent that they would not hearken and obey the Ministers of God, nor God himself. This is a lamentable condition then thou art in: if thine affections be earthly and carnal, the heart is quite hardened to Godward.

Now then my brethren, we see here the reason why ye can refuse to obey, and be divorced from your sins: we see the reason why ye neither

yield to God, nor his Ministers; this is the reason says God, ye are impudent, and your hearts are desperately hardened. And this is the brand the
holy Ghost sets upon you; when your hearts are thus hardened, he calls
you plainly, wicked men and wicked women. "A wicked man hardeneth
his face," Prov. 21.29. Is it not a pitiful thing that a man should go to
hell, and have no remedy to deliver him? To be damned, and have no
remedy in the world to escape it? In such a case is thy soul, whose heart
is thus hardened. "He that being often reproved hardeneth his heart,
shall be destroyed without remedy," Prov. 29.1. Hast thou not been
often reproved? I know thy conscience can tell thee thou hast been often
reproved; hast thou not hardened thy heart? I know thy conscience can
witness that thou wouldest not leave off thy courses; but hast hardened
thy heart to this day, thou knowest I say true; well then, read what a
piteous condition thou art come to, there is no remedy for thee to avoid
the damnation of hell: thou shalt be destroyed without remedy, says
God, I confess there is a remedy, but he shall be destroyed without it.
The remedy that God uses to deliver men from hell, is to reprove them
for their sins, but thou puttest off reproofs, the preaching of the Word,
but thou dost disobey it, the blood of the Lord Jesus, but thou dost defile
it, and wilt not lay down thy corruption for it, there is a remedy but thou
wilt not use it; no, thy heart is hardened and thou shalt be destroyed
without remedy: assure thyself of it, for the mouth of the Lord hath
spoken it.

I speak to you who speak evil of the good way, and call it all to naught;
your hearts are all hardened on this manner: when divers were hardened,
says the Text, and spake evil of that way, Act. 19.9. They that speak
evil of the ways of God are all hardened. O sayst thou, I do but speak
against Puritans and Hypocrites, God forbid I should speak evil of the
ways of the Lord: God forbid, yea, God forbid indeed; but does not thy

conscience witness thou speakest evil of the ways of the Lord? Thou
knowest the Lord commands exhorting and reproofing one another,
and thou speakest evil of it: what hath he to do to reprove me? Sayst
thou. Thou knowest God hath commanded us to walk strictly, and
precisely, and purely, and thou speakest evil of it: what must we be so
pure forsooth? And so precise, and so strict? Thou speakest evil of the
way of the Lord, and the Lord says thou art the man that art hardened.

I speak to you that break the limits of God. God hath commanded
you a great while ago to repent and believe, and cast away the evil of
your doings. Many days are past since ye were called hereto; yesterday,
and today thou art called, and thou amendest not, thou art the man that
is hardened. Again, he limits a certain day after so long a time, as it is said,
today if ye will hear his voice, harden not your hearts, Heb. 4.7. thou hast
broken this limit, and thou art not converted to this day, thou art the
man that is hardened.

I speak to you who refuse to amend your lives: ye do not only not
amend, but also ye refuse to amend, ye are the men that are hardened;
they have made their faces harder then a rock, they have refused to return,
Jer. 5.3. When men refuse to return, they have hardened their hearts
like a rock, and more too, says the Text. Ye have refused, and it is not
unknown to your consciences that ye refuse, therefore ye are the men
that are hardened; ye are the men that shall be destroyed without remedy.
I pray God help you with a remedy, and awaken your souls, that ye may
be hardened no longer; for if ye be, ye shall be destroyed without remedy.

I beseech you consider your poor souls, and understand, if perhaps
ye may find mercy. "Schola cujusque ordinis homines admittit," says
Quintilian, the school admits all sorts of scholars. So I may say of you,
the School of Christ admits all sorts of sinners among you. There is never
a wretch among you all, but if now ye will be content to go to Christ's

school, ye shall be admitted to learn. The Lord give you hearts so to do. O then set your affections on God; the affections are the softness of the heart, and this is the way for to soften them.

The FourteenthSermon

"Set your affections on things that are above, and not on things which are on the earth." – Colossians 3:2

A beginning has been made to persuade you with motives that you would set your affections on God. Five motives have been noted that our Apostle handles in this Chapter: and six motives that the theme itself does afford you. Give me now leave to go on in the same point, and to help you with more. For if this point be not copious with motives, no point can be copious. All persuasion is by moving the affections, whatever the theme be; now when the affections themselves be the theme, the matter of necessity must be copious and abundant: other motives remain to set your affections above.

The first is taken from the everlastingness of the affections, Our affections are everlasting in our soul, especially some of them, and those that are not, when the soul is in hell, the very want of them is a little hell to the soul, for there shall be no joy, no delight, no hope, no comfort, no love; and as the Stomach when it wanteth its meat, it devoureth itself: so these affections, when the matter is wanting, they shall eat up, and devour up the soul. There's no matter in hell to joy at, no matter in hell to delight in, no comfortable matter to hope for, no amiable thing for to love, and this shall vex the soul with weeping and gnashing of teeth: nevertheless, many of the affections, whether a man go to heaven or to hell, are everlasting affections, joy and delight, and love, and all the liking affections shall be everlasting in heaven: fear, and horror, and hatred, and grief, and despair, and shame shall be everlasting in hell, there shall be weeping and gnashing of teeth, says the Text, he does not say there shall be love or joy, &c.

Now are the affections everlasting in the soul? Know this, nothing but God can hold the soul tack, as we say, everlastingly. It's true, we may affect meat for a while, and raiment for a while, and maintenance for a while, and houses, and wives, and husbands, and recreations for a while, till we die, but when death comes, death takes off these objects forever. If thine affections were mainly set upon these things; when these are all gone, alas, where art thou then? Thou art at a loss forever and ever. As Zophar says of the wicked, though he had the world at will while he was living, yet says he, he shall perish forever like his own dung, they which have seen him shall say, where is he? Job. 20:7. Before, he was at his pleasures, and his profits, and his businesses in the world, there he was where his affections did run: but now when his pleasures are all gone, his house, and his lands, and his markets are all gone, alas! Where is he? He is now at a loss, Zophar knew well enough where he is when he dies, he is in hell to be damned and tormented forever; but he expresses it thus, to show that now he is at a loss. Set thine affections then upon grace and upon the fear of the Lord; for though thou diest, this cannot die with thee. It was a good answer of Stilpon, when he lost his country, and his children, and his wife, and his house, and Demetrius said to him, How now Stilpon, where art thou now? Art thou not at a loss now? Ποῦ εἶ;

οὐκέτι; Poo ei? Ouketi? At a loss? Says he, No, no, I have virtue still, and righteousness still: so if thou shouldest lose means and maintenance, friends, stays, hopes, health and all, thou couldest not be at a loss: were thine affections set upon Christ, thou wouldest have thy faith still, thy comfort still, thy peace of conscience still, assurance of heaven still. Thine affections are everlasting, and therefore set thine affections upon such things as are everlasting, otherwise thou shalt be at a loss one day forever and ever.

The second motive is taken from the infiniteness of the affections; the affections are infinite, and therefore nothing in this whole world is able to satisfy them. "He that loveth silver shall never be satisfied with silver, nor he that loveth abundance with increase," Ecclesiastes 5:10. Give him tens, he would be glad with twenties; give him them, he could afford to have hundreds; give him them, he could desire thousands. When he hath thousands, he is never the nearer; nothing satisfies him. Give Alexander a world, he desires another. Take me a silly man, give him a Curateship, he desires a Vicarage; give him that, he desires a Parsonage; give him that, he desires two Benefices; give him that, he desires a Prebendary, an Archdeaconry, and then a Bishopric, and if he were Pope of Rome, he were not satisfied.

Take a voluptuous man, give him pleasure today, he desires more tomorrow, from Cards to the Tables, from them to Bowls, from them to huntings and hawkings, and so on; he is never satisfied till he dies. "Αἱ ἐπιθυμίαι ἄπειροι," says Eustratius, "the affections are infinite even as the fire"; all the forests and all the woods, and all the fuel under heaven can never satisfy the fire; give it faggots, it could burn logs; give it logs, it could burn whole trees; give it trees, it could burn whole houses; give it them, it could burn the inhabitants. Nay, Solomon compares the affections to the fire of hell, and the mouth of the grave, that can never be satisfied. "Hell and destruction are never full; so the eyes of man are never satisfied," Proverbs 27:20. The eye is never satisfied with seeing, the ear is never satisfied with hearing; still, it desires further, "what news?" Proverbs 30:15. He compares them to the Horseleech, "give, give," says the Horseleech; it's ever sucking, more and more, and more; it's ever desiring. The affections are infinite; there's nothing in this world can ever satisfy them.

Did ever any meals meat so satisfy the stomach, that it should never hunger more? Did ever a suit of apparel so satisfy the back, that it should never wish to be clothed more? Did ever Rent so satisfy the Landlord, that he should never desire another day to receive more? The affections are infinite; nothing in the world can ever satisfy them. What good reason then is there to set thine affections upon God? God is infinite, and he can satisfy them. "He filleth the hungry with good things," Luke 1:53. If the affections hunger after God, he will fill them, and satisfy them. If thine affections be set upon God, thou shalt have all satisfaction.

Hath a neighbour wronged thee? Thou needest not seek after revenge; Christ will make thee satisfaction. Hast thou had losses in thy estate, and disgraces in thy name, or troubles in thy mind? Thou needest not disquiet thyself; Christ will make thee satisfaction. "He that complains is not content," as we say; thou needest not complain, saying, "O I have but a poor house to dwell in, poor diet to feed on, poor apparel to put on, poor friends to rely on"; if thine affections be set upon God, look what they want, Christ will make it up, he will satisfy thee. "My people shall be satisfied with goodness," saith the Lord, Jeremiah 31:14. "Thou openest thy hand, and satisfiest the desire of every living thing," Psalm 145:16.

O ye poor souls, that have gone on in your drinkings and carousings, and are never satisfied, that have followed your pleasures, and your vanities, and to this hour ye are not satisfied, what mean you to lose yourselves in the things of this life? What mean you to befool your own souls as ye do? Hear what the Lord Jesus says to you, "Ho, everyone that thirsteth, come to the waters, and he that hath no money, come ye, buy and eat; yea, come, buy wine and milk without money, and without price; wherefore do ye spend money for that which is not bread? And your labour for that which satisfieth not? Hearken diligently to me," says he, "and eat ye that which is good, and let your soul delight itself in fatness," Isaiah 55:1-2. "Ho, everyone that thirsteth, come ye to the waters." What? When ye are athirst will ye go to broken cisterns? They cannot hold water to satisfy you. Here be waters indeed, that Christ does afford you: when ye have money in your purse to buy food, will ye buy that which is not bread? Stones instead of bread? Will ye spend your strength and your health, and your wits, and your pains, and your souls too upon the things of this life? Alas, they can never satisfy you.

"If the fountains should run wine, the people would not be content," as the Proverb is. "Nemo suâ sort contentus est," says the Heathen. Had ye all the beer in the barrels, all the bread at the Bakers, all the corn upon the ground, all the wealth, and riches, and honour in the earth, they can never satisfy you, your souls shall die beggars for all these, and go to hell notwithstanding all these; alas, ye buy them all at a dear rate: do ye not know what they cost Ahab? They cost him himself, he sold himself for them.

Come ye hither, says Christ, set your affections here. Here is mercy for nothing, and grace for nothing, and goodness for nothing, and the Holy Spirit for nothing: can ye desire it at an easier price? Though ye have not one single groat of any worth, not only single farthing or a brass token of any righteousness of your own; yet come hither, says Christ, ye may make as good a market as the best; Come and buy without money, here ye shall have enough to satisfy you. "Bene est cui Deus obtulit," says Boethius: it is happy for you, can ye but see your own happiness, that God gives you such an offer as this.

Here ye may have the pardon of your sins, will that satisfy you? Here ye may have deliverance from hell and condemnation, will that satisfy you? Here ye may have grace against your sins, and power to subdue them; here ye may have the love of God, and the favour of Christ, and the communion of the Spirit, will that satisfy you? I will promise you here is enough to satisfy you, be ye never so unsatisfiable. Here ye may have every manner of thing that is good; comfort against all troubles, sure promises against all doubtings, strength against all weaknesses, stays and props under all sicknesses, assurance of Heaven and a Kingdom as soon as ever ye die, we will warrant you ye shall be satisfied here.

Old Simeon as soon as ever he had Christ in his arms, "Lord, let me now die," says he, q. d. Lord, now I have enough: I care for no more in the whole world now, Lord, now lettest thou thy servant depart in peace: I am well satisfied now I have Christ.

O then set your affections upon God and his Christ, and this will then satisfy you: your affections are infinite, and nothing can give them satisfaction but God that is infinite.

The third motive is taken from the cloyedness of the affections: as the affections are infinite and can never be satisfied with the things of this life, so they are soon cloyed, sometimes affecting, sometimes disaffecting. Nothing can give a man's affections full content but only their God. If thou dost not set thine affections upon God, thine affections can never have content: the things of this life were never made for our affections to be set on; if thine affections were made to be set upon the things of this life, they could never be cloyed with them.

Is the fire ever cloyed with burning? Is a stone ever cloyed with lying on the ground? Is the sun ever cloyed with shining? No, it is made for this end: thou wert never made to eat and to drink, for thy stomach will be cloyed with meat, and cloyed with drinks: the sweetest meats under heaven, if ye burden your stomach therewith, they will cloy it: thou wert never made to hunt and to bowl, to dice, and to card, because thou mayst be cloyed with pleasure; thine affections are subject to a cloy, if they be set upon the things of this life; they are monsters and devils incarnate, that are never weary with swearing, and lying, and playing, and company-keeping. I say, these men are all monsters: for if a man be a man, and he be not a monster, he will be cloyed and wearied with his ways.

They are bad enough that the Prophet does speak of, I am sure they were cursed wretches, yet they were not such-damned wretches as never to be weary with their sins; they have wearied themselves to commit iniquity, Jer. 9:5. They were weary with sinning, and cloyed with their ways, and yet they would on: on they went, but it seems they were not quite monsters to go on and never be wearied, there is nothing in this life thou canst set thine affections upon, but it will weary and cloy thine affections, and therefore without doubt they are not the true objects of thine affections.

What base Proverbs have the wicked, when they come from their sports? Sometimes ye shall hear them say, "I am as weary as a dog"; when the drunkard hath barrelled himself with his liquor, he is as sick as a dog other whiles, as we say; such filthy-mouthed speeches we have, which show they are cloyed now and then with these things; as the Poet says of the Horse and the Ox, "Optat ephippia Bos piger, optat arare caballus," the lazy Ox that is toiling at the Plough, he is weary with it, he could wish he were used like a Horse to the saddle, that would be less wearisome he thinks than the Plough; the Horse that is toiled with its riding, O he is weary with it, he could wish he were used to the yoke, that would be a far easier life. Thus men's ways do weary and cloy their affections: the proud Minion is wearied and cloyed with such an odd fashion, O she must have another; the gamester is wearied with such a kind of sport, he must have another; the delicate palate is cloyed with such tasted meats, it must have others.

Certainly thine affections are wrong set when they are apt to be cloyed in this manner. O therefore set thine affections on God, there thou shalt never be cloyed. I know a man may set his affections to Godward, and be weary, but then they are not right set when he is weary. They served God amiss when they said, behold, what a weariness is it: Mal. 1:13. If they had gone a right way to work, they had never been weary nor cloyed with serving of God. But ye brethren, be not weary with well-doing, 2 Thess. 3:13. that is, set your affections aright upon, and so be never weary with it: the affections will never be cloyed when they are truly set upon God: the flesh will be weary, but the spirit cannot be weary.

God gives the soul full absolute content; the soul is at rest when it is set upon God. As the stone is never cloyed with lying on the ground, because there is its rest, so God is the rest of the soul. The greatest glutton in the world will come at last to say, "I have eaten too much"; the greatest drunkard, "I have drunken too much"; the greatest spend-thrift, "I have spent away too much"; his affections are cloyed: but set thine affections upon God, thou canst never come to too much, never be godly too much, never be heavenly too much, never be in God's favour too much, never in Christ too much, thy spirit can never be cloyed: too much of one thing is good for nothing, say people, it is not needful to be too much pure and too much precise, less would serve the turn: whosoever thou art that canst say or think so, it is sure thou never knewest the meaning of grace.

O say they, does not Solomon say, a man may be too much just, "Be not righteous overmuch, neither make thyself overwise: for why shouldest thou destroy thyself?" Ecc. 7:16. Is it not enough to be weary of goodness, but ye must misconstrue and blaspheme the Word of God too? This is the meaning of Solomon. Solomon never said so himself, but he brings in thy filthy blasphemous mouth thus saying, "Tush, be not thou righteous overmuch, why shouldst thou destroy thyself? Why shouldst thou be so precise, to be called a Puritan, to be hated and reviled, to destroy thine own credit, and thy pleasure, and thy liberty?" Indeed as it follows, "we would not have thee overmuch wicked," &c. verse 17. A little pleasure will do well, a little vanity, a little liberty, a little revenge, a little gain of apparel, a little mirth at the pot will do well; but be not wicked overmuch. I say, these are thy hellish speeches, and none of Solomon's. Solomon does but bring thee in speaking, as the Prophet Isaiah does such as thou, "Let us eat and drink for tomorrow we shall die." O beloved, if ye would set your affections on God, your affections could never be cloyed.

The fourth motive is taken from the preciousness of the affections: the affections are the precious motions of the heart, the heart counts that precious which most it affects. Now what a shame is this, to set thine affections then upon the things of this life? Thou hast a base heart to do so. Hast thou a Kingdom to set thine affections upon? Hast thou a God, and a Christ, and a Crown forever and ever, all glory and honour to set thine affections upon? And wilt thou set thine affections upon dross and dung, and such base things as these? Dost thou not know that all thy vanities and thy pleasures are base in comparison of Christ? All thy silks and thy satins, all thy gentility and thy pomp in the world, are vile in comparison of grace and of glory? Dost thou not know how God scorns all these things in comparison of the excellency of his grace and favour? Thou hast a very base and a vile heart, if thou wilt set thine affections upon these things.

So every wicked man is called a vile person, Psalms 15:4. "The vile person will speak villainy," Isaiah 32:6. Great Nineveh, the Prophet calls it vile, Nahum 1:14. "The vilest men are exalted," Psalm 12:8. If we should see a Lord's son keep company with them that are meaner than is fitting, will ye not say he is base? If we should see how Sadernapalus, a King, would sit spinning and wheeling with the Maids; and Domitian, the Emperor, sit catching flies, and hanging them up, would ye not say they are base? They do things unworthy themselves: themselves should be Noble and Honourable, and Royal, and yet should so vilify and debase their own selves in this fashion. What, a Christian be gaming, and hoyting, that might have joys unspeakable and glorious? A Christian going to Alehouses, or other base places, that might go into the Courts of the Almighty? A Christian complain of the frown of a man whose breath is in his nostrils, that might have the favour of Heaven? A Christian angry at a trifle? A Christian not able to endure the loss of a little earthly silver, that might have all the riches of glory? What a base man is he? What baseness is this in thee? Ah, thou thinkest basely of God, and basely of Christ, and basely of grace, and basely of the Kingdom of Heaven, that settest thine affections more on the dirty and beggarly things of this life, than on Him.

The Proverb of a fool is, "He is penny-wise and pound-foolish": So thou art penny-wise and pound-foolish: wise for the things of this world, and foolish to the things of God. The best things of the earth compared to grace, are no better than a penny to a pound: what a strange thing is this that we should be thus basely foolish? Not affect a Sermon more than a Play; not affect the grace of our Lord Jesus Christ more than an earthly bargain. There is a homely saying, but it is a most true one. "A Fool will not give his bawble for the Tower of London": his affections are more on his Hat and his Feather, than on anything else, he is very serious about ridiculous things. Fie for shame brethren, let us not be so profanely conceited of grace, so basely minded as to set our affections here below, when we are called to set them on God.

The fifth motive is taken from the instability of our affections: if our affections be set upon the things of this life, they must be fain to repent of it at last, whatever come of it: whether we be saved or damned, it is certain we shall repent of it: if ever thou go to Heaven, God will make thee repent that ever thou hast been so vain, so carnal, so voluptuous, so proud; God will make thy heart ache for it. "I abhor myself," says Job, "and repent in dust and ashes," Job 42:6. O I could even spit in mine own face, I could even be content to gnash my teeth at mine own soul, that ever I sinned thus and thus, now I repent it in dust and ashes, O that I had never done so; were it to do again, I would never do it for a thousand worlds: thus if thou go to heaven thou wilt be fain to repent it. And if thou go to hell, thine own horror and thine intolerable torments and plagues will force thee to repent it too, that ever thou hast set thine affections on earth; then thou wilt curse thine own self, and ban thine own thoughts, and fret and stamp at thine own madness, that thou shouldest set thine affections upon the things of the world, when thou mightest have had a Saviour, and a God, if thou hadst been wise and wouldest have been ruled. "Magni emitur poenitentia," alas, such repentance costeth thee dear. When it hath cost thee thy soul and brought thee to hell, and utterly undone thee forever, then thou learnest how to repent. When Dives was in hell, then he repented that ever he was so hard-hearted to Lazarus: "Send Lazarus, &c." O he would now ask him forgiveness; send such a poor wretch now, I will make him restitution. "Lord send now thy commandments, and now we will obey them; Lord, now send thy Ministers unto us, and we will hear them; send us one Sermon more, and now we will do it." As sure as God is in Heaven, you will repent it another day, that ever you set your affections thus on the things of this life. Beloved, were it not better by odds, not to set your affections thus at all, then when ye have done it, repent it, when all comes to all? "Non admiseris cuius postea paeniteat." Do not commit that if ye be wise, which ye must repent when ye have done it. This very Sermon, if ye will not hearken now to obey it, I say this very Sermon your consciences will be sure to vex you withal. "Such a Sermon I heard, and there I had a warning, then I was told of this vengeance I endure, but I would not listen. O woe is me and my rebellion, that I did not." I beseech you consider it, set your affections otherwise than ye do, set them graciously on God, or else ye will be forced to repent forever.

The sixth motive is taken from the jealousy of the affections: Beloved, when a Husband suspects his wife's affections are not to him, there is an affection of jealousy arises in his heart to revenge it: a man cannot abide that his wife should give her affections to another. So beloved, God is a jealous God, when he sees he cannot have thy affections to him: he hath made thee his creature, he hath hired thee for his servant, nay he espoused thy soul as a wife and a Spouse to his own Son; and if he may suspect that thy affections are otherwise set, he will be jealous against thee. This will be the grievousest revenge of all revenges that are possible. No revenge like the revenge for the turning ones affections awry. Let a man be wronged though never so much, nothing but anger and choler does arise to revenge it; but if he suspect the want of affection in his own wife, then it is not an anger alone that arises to revenge it, but a jealousy. Dost thou not know what jealousy is? I tell you, it is the revengefullest passion that ever arose in the breast. Jealousy is the rage of a man, therefore he will not spare in the day of vengeance; he will regard no ransom, neither will he rest content, though thou givest many gifts, Proverbs 6:34, 35. We have a good Proverb, "From jealousy the good Lord deliver us," Ἀπόφθονον, says Oppia, "The heart of jealousy is wild and all savage." A man is not only angry, but directly in a rage, that is jealous, So God expresses himself by a fury and a rage, saying, "my fury shall break out against them, and I will not pity them." When thine affections go a whoring from God, he will be revenged on thee deeply; he will take no ransom; no ransom by Christ, no ransom in the world: couldest thou give him a whole world for the sin of thy soul, he will not accept it. What says the Husband when he is jealous, "what hast thou defiled my bed and played the whore?" and so forth. I will make you an example: he eats himself up, till he is revenged: he will mark every cast of her eye, every gesture of her body, every tread of her foot, every thing now shall be matter of suspicion: she shall not speak to any man in the street, but he will suspect it is wantonness; She shall not be able to go one step out of doors, but he will suspect it is to her base lovers. So if we set our affections wrong upon other things besides God, God will never put it up at our hands. He will then be extreme to mark whatsoever is amiss; not one idle word, but he will be precise to observe it; not one vain thought, but he will be curious to note it; not one foolish fashion, but he will set it down in his note-book, he will then be extreme with thee. Ye have read and heard the Ten Commandments often and often. Ye know what is said in the second Commandment, "Thou shalt not do thus and thus," For I the Lord thy God am a jealous God, and visit the sins of the fathers upon the children. If thou set up these Idols in thy heart, to affect the things of this life, take heed of this jealousy, I the Lord thy God am a jealous God, &c. He will visit not only thy sins upon thee, but he will look what thy father hath done, and thy grandfather hath done, and thy great grandfather hath done. If any of them have been drunkards, he will visit it on thee: if any of them have been swearers and worldlings, and wicked, he will visit it on thee. From his jealousy the good Lord deliver us.

The seventh motive is taken from the tyranny of our affections if they are not set right. If our affections are not set upon God, they are the sorest tyrants that can be to tyrannize over us. Philo compares the tyranny of our affections to the four hundred years' bondage of the Israelites in Egypt. You remember what woeful and slavish bondage they were put to in Egypt, insomuch that they groaned under it, and cried out unto God. Pharaoh played the Tiger-like Tyrant over them, and made them weary of their lives: so do the affections tyrannize over a man that is carnal and earthly, they do so besot him, and befool him, that he knows not how to come out of his sins; they do so harden him and obdurate him, that no preaching nor counsel can convert him; they do so occupy and task him, and busy him, that he can find no while to save his own soul, or bethink himself of escaping of hell and damnation, he is in hell before ever he thinks on it seriously; they plague him like Tantalus, says he, and leave his soul in the lurch after all his vain hopes, he can never be free for God.

The Apostle speaking of the lust and affections of the world, how they allure men into vanity; he says they promise men liberty, but they are the servants and slaves of corruption. 2 Peter 2:19. A man would wonder how one should be in bondage with a pot or a pipe, with a bowl or a game, with a carnal friend, or an use he hath gotten; but so it is, that nor Minister, nor Sermon, nor warnings from God, nor anything can free him: still he is enthralled. Now consider, are our affections such tyrants, when they are set upon the things of this life? O let us set them upon God. If they can captivate us to God, and bring us into a golden bondage with grace and with goodness, we are happy.

Seest thou how the wicked are tied to their sins, and their lusts? So if thine affections were set upon God, thou wouldest be tied unto God. O it's an admirable tie, this, to be tied unto God. This is it that the wisest man in the earth adviseth us to, "My son," says he, "keep thy father's commandments, bind them continually upon thy heart, and tie them about thy neck," Proverbs 6:21. Thine affections are these stay-bands, and these typers: if thine affections are set upon the Word, they will tie it to thy soul; if they are set upon grace, and love to God's Ordinances, his Sabbaths and his ways, they will tie them to thy heart: if thou wilt not set thine affections upon God, thou art a very slave, a very slave unto Satan and to sin; thou art not only in a woeful condition, as thou art, but they tie thee fast to it; and if God may not be so much beholden to thee for thine affections to himward, he will entrap thee, and take thee by them, as a Bare is taken by a Collar, and hale thee to judgment.

Thou hast little affection or none at all to the Word; maybe thou comest not to be reproved and amended by the Word, but thou comest to have some knowledge, and some pretty sentence to talk on, or some fine story or passage to speak on: "As I live," saith the Lord, "I will answer thee according to thy thoughts": maybe thou comest that thou mayst scrape up some hopes to have mercy, and heaven at the last; maybe thou comest to snatch up some sentence or other that may secure up thy conscience: if there be ever a passage of mercy, that thou wouldest fain have; "As I live," saith the Lord, "I will answer thee according to thy thoughts, and thine own vain heart": that which thou camest for in the Word, "as I live," saith the Lord, thou shalt have it. Thou dost not come to learn how to be holy and be stricter than thou art, but though thou beest no stricter than thou art already, yet to have some hopes to be saved for all that.

FINIS.